THE LONDON
LS

THE LONDON
LS

Pen & Sword
TRANSPORT

MATTHEW WHARMBY

Cover: **Bromley's LS 103 (OJD 903R) shows just why single-deckers have always been the 227's only stock; the low bridge at Shortlands. New in 1977, it is seen during October 1979 and survives today in preservation.** *R. C. Riley*

Rear cover, top: **A comparison between the original design of Leyland National and its latter-day upgrade (as the National 2) can be seen when Peckham's LS 224 (THX 224S) passes Victoria's LS 468 (GUW 468W) as the pair enter Victoria bus station on 28 October 1985.** *R. C. Riley*

Rear cover, middle: **Devolution of London Transport in the 1980s brought a new 'tapegrey' livery and new fleetnames, not to mention new deployments for the LS class as their original routes were converted to minibus operation. Chalk Farm received LS 101 (OJD 901R) among others to convert the 214 when its Titans were needed elsewhere, and during 1989 it is captured on its way through Camden Town.** *Peter Horrex*

Rear cover, bottom: **As London Buses Ltd gave way to the private sector, its last move with its National 2s was to commission their comprehensive rebuilding as National Greenways, buying them another decade in service. Seen at Victoria on 3 July 2001, GLS 502 (GUW 502W) is a London General bus operating out of the dedicated Red Arrow base at Waterloo.** *Matthew Wharmby*

Title page: **Your basic London Transport Leyland National, whose only difference from the manufacturer's rigid standard specification was in the fitment of moquette seats; everything else, from blinds to paintwork to numberplates was all Leyland. LS 318 (AYR 318T), coming into South Harrow bus station, was new to Harrow Weald in August 1979 and on 31 August 1982 was still working from there.** *John Laker*

DEDICATION

To Mum

First published in Great Britain in 2018 by
PEN & SWORD TRANSPORT

An imprint of
Pen & Sword Books Ltd
Yorkshire – Philadelphia
Copyright © Matthew Wharmby

ISBN 978 1 47386 227 2

The right of Matthew Wharmby to be identified as Author of this work has been asserted by him in accordance with the Copyright, Designs and Patents Act 1988.

A CIP catalogue record for this book is available from the British Library

Typeset by Matthew Wharmby
Printed and bound by Replika Press Pvt. Ltd.

Pen & Sword Books Ltd incorporates the Imprints of Aviation, Atlas, Family History, Fiction, Maritime, Military, Discovery, Politics, History, Archaeology, Select, Wharncliffe Local History, Wharncliffe True Crime, Military Classics, Wharncliffe Transport, Leo Cooper, The Praetorian Press, Remember When, Seaforth Publishing and Frontline Publishing.

For a complete list of Pen & Sword titles please contact

PEN & SWORD BOOKS LTD
47 Church Street, Barnsley, South Yorkshire, S70 2AS, England
E-mail: enquiries@pen-and-sword.co.uk
Website: www.pen-and-sword.co.uk

Or
PEN AND SWORD BOOKS
1950 Lawrence Rd, Havertown, PA 19083, USA
E-mail: Uspen-and-sword@casematepublishers.com
Website: www.penandswordbooks.com

CONTENTS

INTRODUCTION

Until comparatively recently, the full-size single-decker occupied a distinctly second tier of importance in London, and indeed nationwide. Anxious to maximise capacity as best it could, London Transport standardised on double-deckers unless clearances both in height and width precluded them, but in 1966 resolved to 'reshape' bus travel altogether to curb a long period of decline. Traffic-choked trunk routes would be curtailed and replaced at their outer ends by flat-fare shuttles operated by multi-standee single-deck routes with buses designed to be one-man-operated and thus save the cost of the second member of staff. Accordingly, 665 Merlins and 838 Swifts were taken into LT stock between 1966 and 1972, but passengers resented both the inhospitable nature of standing and having to change buses all the time, and the decline continued, if anything accelerated by the sheer unreliability of the new buses.

At the same time, Leyland Motors had gradually acquired or taken over most of the country's bus manufacturing and bodying concerns and set out to assimilate their designs into a one-size-fits-all double-decker and single-decker alike. The latter incorporated advanced manufacturing concepts inspired by the car industry to produce the National, designed to complement the state-owned National Bus Company that, under the Transport Act of 1968, took over and standardised both the BET and Tilling groups.

Outside London, the National garnered considerable resentment for its part in sidelining established AEC, Leyland and Daimler models as well as its participation in the rebranding of traditional companies into the austere NBC, but in the capital, what became the LS class was received almost as a miracle. Here, after so long, was a genuinely reliable, if thoroughly unglamorous workhorse that just did the job asked of it without any fuss, and London Transport liked them enough to become the country's major operator, taking 506 of them between 1973 and 1981. Of these, the last 69 were of the improved Leyland National 2 design.

The LSs settled down to do the ten years demanded of them without fanfare, carrying on amid the great upheaval that transformed London Transport into London Buses Ltd and its twelve subsidiaries, and then began departing at the end of the 1980s as minibuses took over their routes. But even then, as recession gripped the country and LBL prepared for privatisation, the National still had a role to play in London. Having seen how increasingly elderly examples had held the fort during the early days of deregulation, LBL got in on the game by refurbishing for a song its National 2s, turning them into the GLS class of National Greenways. And after that, London United, one of the post-LBL privatised operators, put its long-serving remnant of LSs through a simpler refurbishment programme that allowed them to continue in service as far as 1999.

Perhaps the valedictory of the otherwise unsung LS class is that as late as 2007, two dozen former London Transport examples could still be seen in everyday service in Walsall with Chase Coaches, with little more than an engine change and a single-door conversion (and sometimes not even that) belying thirty years of unbroken service.

This is the LSs' story in the capital. Thanks of course are due to all photographic contributors, to my editor and to the publisher for allowing the story to be told.

Matthew Wharmby
Walton-on-Thames, Surrey
May 2017

Above: **The era covered by this book spans unprecedented change to London's buses. When this photograph of Norbiton's LS 273 (YYE 273T) was taken at Staines in 1980, London Transport was unassailable, if long fallen from its halcyon days.** *Haydn Davies*

Left: **Two decades later, LT was gone, its constituents sold to the private sector. The LSs had achieved their expected decade and a bit, but the straitened financial conditions of the time prompted reconditioning of surviving Nationals, in order to make astute tendering bids. London United thus enjoyed three more years out of its LSs, and here at Hounslow on 20 February 1999 is LS 385 (BYW 385V).** *Author*

CHAPTER ONE

ANTECEDENTS

Below: **Tough as nails, the RF racked up 28 years in London service, serving on both red and green routes and as buses and coaches. LT spun their service out as long as it could, knowing that any successor would have its work cut out. Here is Uxbridge's RF 324 (MXX 295) on 16 June 1972 at Hayes; the 204 would subsequently spend most of a decade with LSs.**
John Laker

London Transport was distinctly spoiled by the RF – rugged and almost indestructible, the 700-strong AEC Regal family was so good that it would prove difficult to replace. It was even adaptable to one-man operation (OMO), the latest hope that would tackle the twin hydras of rising costs and falling patronage suffered during the 1960s. But by the time the Reshaping Plan came along, the RFs were in middle age and even the Green Line modernisation several of them went through was only a stopgap; the new order would need specially-designed buses. Impressed by the undoubtedly successful Red Arrow route 500 introduced in 1966 with standee AEC Merlins, LT unfortunately made the fatal error of assuming that suburban passengers, as distinct from West End commuters, wouldn't mind standing up during their carriage along curtailed routes anchored on interchange hubs. To make the standee-OMO concept pay for itself, it had to be extended as far fleetwide and as quickly as legislation could be written and rewritten to accommodate it. Routemaster deliveries came gently to their close and large orders for Merlins were placed.

Above: **In accordance with the tenets of the Reshaping Plan that promised to alleviate its perennial staffing problems, London Transport ploughed ahead with single-deck OMO, but aside from the alienation of passengers by such extreme changes, the vehicles selected came up terribly short. There were two generations of AEC Swift-based flat-fare single-deckers, the latter forming the SM and SMS classes of 838 buses in total, and here in Chiswick on 11 August 1978 is SMS 804 (JGF 804K) out of Turnham Green. The E3 was converted to LS operation on 17 September 1978 and ran them until 1981.** *John Laker*

The first wave of Reshaping bowed on 7 September 1968 and was immediately in trouble; the passengers didn't appreciate the risk of embarrassment if the automatic fareboxes into which they now had to drop an exact fare failed to release the turnstiles, only to have to stand up thereafter, often with heavy shopping and children in tow. They already knew they didn't like to change buses on one journey if they could help it, and nor did they appreciate being made to pay twice or more even if their previous through routes had become hopelessly snarled by traffic. The sheer unreliability of the MB and MBS classes didn't help, and they were too long for London streets. After 665 were in service, LT switched to the shorter version, taking up the Swift name that properly applied to either length of chassis, and introduced the SMs and SMSs, 838 of which entered service up to early 1972. These were no improvement; the shorter body came with a correspondingly derated engine, which struggled to pull the heavy weight and indeed contributed to the buses' deforming in the middle. Delicensing of failed buses reached epic proportions, exacerbated by a nationwide spares shortage and continuous spates of industrial action.

After the last SMSs were delivered, thoughts passed towards future single-deck purchases despite double-deckers, in the form of the DMS at this point, having come back into the ascendancy. The Leyland National was well on its way to supplanting the products of Leyland's one-time competitors that it had progressively acquired, and its ease of construction, promising timely delivery, made it an obvious choice. At the same time, dissatisfaction with Leyland's near-monopoly as it had effectively become since the falling away of orders for AEC buses, prompted hitherto unprecedented looks at foreign manufacturers. The Metro-Scania of Swedish chassis but carrying an MCW body had already seen service in London when VWD 451H spent part of 1970 on the 99 out of Plumstead, so in 1972 LT hedged its bets and ordered six of each. While LT waited, an example of the Leyland National (in LT red) was looked over at the start of 1973 but LT pronounced dissatisfaction with the gearbox and requested modifications, which were added to the demonstrator before it went away, and subsequently incorporated in the six LSs.

The Metro-Scanias, classified MS 1-6, seated B37D+29 and were the first to carry LT's new livery incorporating a considerable proportion of white. They were delivered between May and July 1973 and entered service on the testbed route, Dalston's S2, on 15 August. A little later came LS 1-6, London Transport's first Leyland Nationals.

THE DALSTON EXPERIMENTALS

After a lifetime of painstakingly-designed bespoke-built buses constructed for interchangeability and longevity, followed by unhappy attempts to convince manufacturers to graft on familiar London Transport-spec components to existing provincial designs, the Leyland National was the opposite extreme, the factory-standard product *par excellence*; you got what you were given and you liked it. Thus did LT receive unfamiliar new examples of technology and equipment, for instance its first three-track number blinds at front and rear, though nothing was displayed on the side to the dismay of passengers, who lobbied LT unsuccessfully to have at least some destination information retrofitted. The numberplates were the stark new black-on-white versions experimented with as avant-garde but now made standard by the DVLC, and even the colour was off

Above: **Dalston's LS 6 (TGY 106M) shows off the nearside treatment of the first six LSs. This one has managed to stay out of Clapton Pond itself!**
Haydn Davies

a Leyland paint swatch and thus not quite standard with existing LT buses, being a little darker. The only concession to LT's identity and continuity at all was the seat moquette, the blue and green-based version current to DMSs and 1972 Underground stock. Further concessions to familiar practice were a LT-spec cab door and the new G2 transmission. To 10.3m length, capacity was B36D+27 and in LT's engineering system were coded 1LS1.

Although the new LSs were destined to carry a version of the new livery phased in from 1973, with a significant proportion of white as the secondary colour, LT had to apply the white themselves; it covered the area above the windows. The roof pod was grey; LS 2 was delivered with a white roof pod but was amended prior to entry into service. LSs 1-6 had the registrations MYK 101-106L booked for them, but their late delivery caused these marks to be voided and they entered service licensed with TGY 101-106M.

Delivered in ones and twos (LS 1 in July, LS 2 in August, LSs 4 and 6 in September and LSs 3 and 5 in October), LSs 1-6 entered service on Dalston's S2 on 19 November 1973, three months after their Metro-Scania counterparts. Although no comparable first-day dives into Clapton Pond were suffered, LS 3, at the same location on its own first day, struck in succession a car, a van and a motorbike! As the buses needed to go back and forth to Aldenham for attention, an element of MBS operation was retained on the S2, and indeed in May 1974 five Merlins were transferred into Dalston to offset teething troubles to both the LS and MS classes, though their fitment with LS blinds meant no route numbers could be displayed.

In spite of noise reduction insisted upon by LT, the LSs' external noise was unmistakable, whining at idle rather than chug-chugging, combined with the harsh puff of air released to flick open its four-leaf doors (two identical sets of which folded to the sides in each doorway). From time to time the buses would exhale to themselves, earning from enthusiasts the sobriquet 'dish', which was rather kinder than the 'Nasty' nickname known everywhere else!

CHAPTER THREE

THE HOUNSLOW BATCH

Two years after the S2's treatment to LSs, it was announced in October 1975 that London Transport had taken up the option on a batch of 51 Leyland Nationals ordered by the transport authority of Caracas, Venezuela but subsequently cancelled. That city would amass a total of 450 Nationals, becoming the largest export market ahead of Jamaica (125 examples) and Trinidad & Tobago (40). Export totals would prove disappointing for Leyland despite the model going on to rack up about 15,000 units built altogether. As in the UK, isolated operations operated their Nationals for close to thirty years.

Authorised by the GLC on 16 December 1975 and expected from April 1976, LSs 51-57 were intended not as a harbinger of future generations of single-deck buses but as an emergency plugging of the still severe spares and availability situation, and it was envisaged that they could just as easily be disposed of as could an equivalent number of Swifts once the problems had eased. To that end, the batch would be allocated *en bloc* to Hounslow, where LSs 1-6 would join them in due course; all would replace SMSs for transfer to the hardest-hit such operating garages. Total outlay came to £1.3m including tools, spares and a little structural work to Hounslow garage.

Broadly to the same spec as their predecessors, LSs 7-57 began arriving in May 1976 and training commenced at Hounslow; the first numbered of these was one of the buses on display at LT's Gala Day at Syon Park on the 16th. Despite deliveries overrunning the August year-letter change, all retained their

Below: **LS 17 (KJD 517P) entered service at Hounslow in August 1976. It is seen at the 110's Twickenham stand in September.** *Tony Wilson*

booked registration marks spanning KJD 507-557P. None were able to be fitted with automatic fare collection equipment, the buses operating as conventional OMO vehicles on Hounslow's routes, and this time the livery was plain red with white filled roundels and fleetnumbers. The London Transport code was 2LS2.

On 13 June 1976 both the LS and MS complement of the S2 were stood down and the route was converted to SMS operation; both Nationals and Metro-Scanias were placed in store.

Entry of LSs 7-57 into service at Hounslow was phased over several weekends; on 15 August the 116 and 257 were converted, followed on the 22nd by routes 110 and 111 and on the 29th by the 203 and 203A, though in practice the suffixed variant was effectively withdrawn due to the inability of the new buses to display the 'A' letter; similar troubles at London Country had obliged the wholesale renumbering of several suffixed routes. On 19 September the A1 express received its new LSs, followed on the 26th by the 81, and finally, on 3 October, the 82 followed suit, completing the conversion. After a period in store, mostly at Mortlake, LSs 1-6 had their fareboxes replaced by a cab-mounted Almex E ticket machine and were transferred to Hounslow in October, by which time the whole batch of LS 7-57 was in service, but the Metro-Scanias, following cancellation of a plan to send them to Peckham for the P3, would linger for two years until sale in 1978; only MS 4 survives in preservation.

On 29 November LT announced its plans for vehicle purchase in the immediate future; as well as 450 double-deckers, 210 single-deckers were envisaged and all were intended to be

Above: **Long before the extension of the Piccadilly Line to Heathrow Airport, there was the A1, taking onward passengers from the line's Hounslow West terminus of the time. It was converted from SMS to LS operation on 19 August 1976 and in October Hounslow's LS 32 (KJD 532P) is seen about to leave Hounslow West station.** *Tony Wilson*

Leyland Nationals. However, illustrating the increasing interference of politicians, the GLC asked LT for more information on 13 December, its transport committee recommending the immediate purchase of only fifty until LT could supply more information about vehicle reliability. In the interim, recertifications would be carried out on the best of the SMSs, buying them the time afforded by a four-year CoF. Whatever the future foretold for LSs, it would be marked by the withdrawal of the SMSs come what may, and withdrawals of long-term disused members of the SM family had already begun.

Left: **In concert with the other five, LS 2 (TGY 102M) was transferred to Hounslow in October 1976, and not long after that is seen plying the 81.** *Haydn Davies*

CHAPTER FOUR

MAIN DELIVERIES

When GLC approval was gained to order and pay for the balance of the 160 Leyland Nationals, it was envisaged that they would replace Swifts on routes restricted by length and width to single-deck operation, while double-deckers would take over where there were no such restrictions, as DMSs had been doing with the Merlins. These comprised routes 12A, 90, 108, 115/115A, 210, 218, 219, 236, 248/248A, 254, 268, 289, E3, H1, P1, P2, S2 and S3; the P3 was also included due to the level of vandalism sustained while it had been double-deck, while the 235, it was thought, could be double-decked if a minor diversion was carried out. In due course all of these would go on to operate LSs, but at the present moment, the fifty confirmed deliveries (LSs 58-107, registered OJD 858-907R) were earmarked for the 12A at Elmers End and the 227 at Bromley, both in replacement of SMSs.

Deliveries commenced in March 1977 and training commenced, though the intended 8 May date of the 12A's conversion was postponed to 19 June. All fifty were in stock by then and the 227 was treated on 21 August, that route's own date having also slipped, but only by a week. It could have been more, had protests by residents along the three roads that led to the 227's stand at Chislehurst been any more vociferous than they already were; a run over the route by LS 80 on 22 July was held up by the residents, who blocked the road and refused to let the National past until they had handed over a petition outlining their concerns over the weight of the new vehicles (8t 13cwt (8788kg) as opposed to 7t 16cwt (7925kg, Park Royal-bodied SMSs) or 7t 19cwt (8077kg, MCW-bodied SMSs)). The trouble was, drivers at Bromley had threatened to strike unless their notoriously unreliable SMSs were replaced at

Right: **The first deployment of 1977 was to the 12A, commencing on 19 June. LS 84 (OJD 884R) was put into service at Elmers End in June 1977 and would spend the next six years there.** *Haydn Davies*

Above: **LS 98 (OJD 898R) emerges from foliage at Chislehurst after entering service on Bromley's 227 in August 1977, but in this instance is going no further west than Penge. This is one of the LSs that can be seen in preservation today.**
Haydn Davies

the earliest convenience! Chislehurst Labour Party lined up with the locals and the union with the busmen, stating that resiting the terminus (perhaps to the Edgebury Estate, as suggested by the residents) was the council's responsibility. In due course the route was pulled out of the side streets to stand by the Gordon Arms. Two of the fifty were licensed at Hounslow but made their way in due course to Bromley (LS 65) and Elmers End (LS 89). For some reason the 'A' on the 12A's third track was white on blue, like that of the A1.

Finally, in July, the GLC signed off on the other 160 LSs and from November they started coming off the lines at Workington. Registered THX 108-267S, LSs 108-267 would be like-for-like Swift replacements. The year was rounded off by repaints to LSs 1-6 at Hounslow; they lost their unique livery accoutrements but at least were now in the 'correct' shade of red! LS 118 was the 5000th production Leyland National. And finally for 1977, the A1 was withdrawn on 17 December now that the Piccadilly Line was running through to Heathrow.

Left: **On 28 January 1978 the 111 was extended from Hampton Station to Kingston. Before that, LS 6 (TGY 106M) from the original batch is in charge.**
Haydn Davies

Right: **As 1978 got going in earnest, the 248 and 248A out of Hornchurch were converted from SMS to LS operation. LS 129 (THX 129S) is carrying the Multi-Ride stickers in use in the area, denoting a fares network whereby a strip of ten cancellable tickets enabled both passenger savings and increased speed of boarding.** *Haydn Davies*

Busplan was the watchword for 1978, a Conservative-inspired rationalisation of route workings in the interests of simplifying operating patterns for passengers' benefit rather than that of the operator. Prior to that, however, the first of the LS 108-267 batch was put into service at Hounslow on 28 January to furnish an unusual scheme whereby the paths of RM-operated trunk route 117 and BL-operated suburban 237 were swapped so that the 117 became a local service with LSs, going no further east than Brentford. To give it a hand the 203 was extended there from Hounslow, although this route lost its Ashford journeys at the same time. Further to the south the 111 was extended from Hampton to Kingston over the roads taken by its Saturday-only projection, as a more regular service than the 264, which was withdrawn and its section beyond the GLC border devolved to a local operator. On the deficit side, however, the 110 was withdrawn on Sundays.

On 5 February 1978 the 268 was converted from SM to LS operation, Cricklewood receiving seven new Nationals. This stood in for the 235, the conversion of which had to wait another year. On the 26th so followed Hornchurch's 248 and 248A, both losing SMSs. The LSs into Hornchurch accompanied the introduction of the Multi-Ride ticketing system based on the

Right: **On 9 April 1978 Fulwell's route 90 was converted from SMD to LS operation with buses like LS 140 (THX 140S). In this case, the blind boxes have been masked down to one line.** *Haydn Davies*

Above: **What is now North Greenwich was still industrial in 1978 when LS 151 (THX 151S) was photographed passing through. Poplar's 108 was converted to LS operation on 22 April.** *Haydn Davies*

London Borough of Havering, but had just one canceller (behind the driver) to the DMSs' two. Fulwell then received its first LSs on 9 April with the conversion of the 90 from the thoroughly unpopular SMD variant of the AEC Swift.

Busplan 78's first stage (of an eventual three) kicked off on 22 April; while that day saw the purge of the knot of RT-operated routes anchored on Lewisham, another important local route was introduced to the LS in the form of the 108, operated by Poplar garage and hitherto with SMs.

On 21 May (though in practice from the 18th as vehicles arrived) the 236, shared between Leyton and Dalston, was converted from SMS to LS, followed on 18 June by another shared route, the 210 predominantly from Muswell Hill but with a minority Holloway allocation daily. Most of the LSs into Muswell Hill were new to Dalston but replaced there by newer deliveries. The next conversion came on 22 July in the form of Loughton's 254. By the autumn, Leyton was putting the odd LS out on SM-operated 235, thanks to the introduction of blinds covering both the 235 and 236 after a period with temporary destination-only sets produced by Aldenham. There were black-on-yellow panels for selected workings, a state of affairs also applying to LS blinds at

Left: **LS 203 (THX 203S) was allocated new to Dalston in May 1978 and is captured in outer Hackney during that month, but in June it was transferred to Muswell Hill.** *Haydn Davies*

Right: **Unlike its Ealing-area flat fare partners, the E3 had to remain single-deck, and LSs were specified when it came time to replace the SMSs. LS 236 (THX 236S) was allocated to Turnham Green on 17 September 1978, at which point Hanwell and Turnham Green had eleven workings each.** *Haydn Davies*

Hornchurch and Loughton. And speaking of yellow on black, running number cards of this colour combination were now the standard and spread across the fleet during 1978.

After slippage of two weeks, 17 September witnessed the conversion of the E3 at Hanwell and Turnham Green from SMS to LS; the E1 and E2 had already received DMSs but the E3, by far the busiest partner in the Ealing E-route network, had a low bridge along line of route.

Then, on 22 October, the H1 at Harrow Weald received new LSs.

During October a local initiative at Hounslow to absorb disruption caused by traffic attending the Sunday morning market at Brentford saw one LS added over the Hounslow-Gunnersbury section of the 237, though with locally-produced windscreen slipboards.

Busplan stage 2 bowed on 28 October 1978. One of its planks involved the reallocation of the

Right: **During October 1978 Hounslow's LS 50 (KJD 550P) is seen on a crowd-busting service mounted to service the Brentford Sunday market and otherwise paralleling the 237. Slipboards a-plenty are in evidence.** *Haydn Davies*

110 from Hounslow to Fulwell. The 289 was also scheduled to be converted from SMS to LS upon its reallocation from Thornton Heath to Elmers End, but due to the insistence by Elmers End's drivers that any incoming LSs were fitted with laminated windscreens, following instances of shattering on the garage's incumbent Nationals (with one injury resulting), SMSs were drafted hurriedly back into Elmers End after the type had previously been withdrawn from there. Enough new LSs had windscreens laminated to the staff's satisfaction and the conversion proceeded on 4 November. On that day Peckham's P3 began trading its SMSs for LSs, again this conversion drifting a week from its intended implementation date. New route P5 was introduced with LSs from the outset on 4 November, combining and replacing the operations of formerly SMS-operated locals P1 and P2. An accident to LS 84 that month, whereby it ran into a house in Croydon, caused substantial distortion to the body that had to be dealt with at Aldenham.

At this point thirty more LSs were ordered; their most significant deployment was to be the 218 and 219, the two remaining RF-operated services. Deliveries commenced in December and all of LSs 268-297 (YYE 268-297T) were in stock by February 1979. Leyton's 235 was intended for conversion from SM to LS on 15 January 1979 but this was postponed due to problems with the new deliveries that had to be sorted out, though one LS from an existing intake turned out.

On 19 March 1979 the 110 became the first LS route to lose the type when a double-deck conversion using new Ms was felt more expedient; the Metrobuses had taken their time arriving and it was only two months after the original date that enough were in stock to pull this off. Of the displaced Fulwell LSs, two went to Norbiton and one each to Holloway, Leyton and Dalston.

The 31st of that month saw the poignant retirement of the last RFs after a 28-year service career; their last two routes, the 218 and 219, could not, however, accommodate LSs at their Kingston garages so both were reallocated to Norbiton using a proportion of the 30-strong order spanning LSs 268-297. Also on that day, long-standing route 254 was withdrawn and its LSs retained to commence two new services that effectively split it in two; the 250 between Waltham Cross and Limes Farm Estate and the 255 between Loughton Station and South Woodford. The balance of the small LS order entered service at Leyton between 3-7 April, replacing SMs on the 235.

Below: **Loughton's LS 194 (THX 194S) has taken a blow to the front when sighted picking its way round the Limes Farm shortly after the introduction of new route 250, but soldiers on nonetheless.** *Haydn Davies*

Early in 1979 140 more Nationals were ordered. Mindful of the slow deliveries of new Metrobuses and Titans (particularly the latter, beset at Park Royal by industrial action), LT envisaged using LSs 298-437 to take over several double-deck OMO routes as their existing DMSs suffered CoF expiry and could not otherwise be overhauled or recertified fast enough; some may have seen this as a demotion, but the LSs were all that was available right now and were more than adequate for the task ahead of them. Even so, LT was busy enough to have to subcontract the finishing of the vehicles once they started arriving in May; the application of yellow paint over the entrance doors plus the affixing of roundels and transfers was allotted to Willowbrook and Wadham Stringer. With an eye on the future, LS 1 was taken into Aldenham in May for a pilot overhaul; LS 7 went in for repaint in September, commencing

the class's routine repainting programme. The LS was represented in the parade in Hyde Park on 8 July by LS 212.

Thus on 25 June did Poplar's 173 and Muswell Hill's 244, both operated by DMSs, receive their new Nationals. The 173 was selected as on 1 September it was going to be extended to Stratford under a low bridge at West Ham, while the 244's passenger loadings did not really merit double-deckers so the loss of its CoF-expired Fleetlines would not be missed. Over the summer, meanwhile, Harrow Weald embarked upon concerted SMS replacement, taking LSs to cover the 209 (19 July) 258 (20 July), 182 on Sundays (22 July), 136 (2 August) and 114 (2 August-3 September). Two of these summer conversions were subjected to alterations on 1 September, the 136 being rerouted in Harrow away from Long Elmes and the 173 gaining a useful extension from Canning

Town to Stratford. The delay in their intended deployment was due to Aldenham having to supply simplified blinds at short notice, as the proper plastic ones had not arrived from the printers; they just featured destinations on two lines. Plastic material was selected for LS blinds as the buses' winding mechanism tended to damage Aldenham's traditional muslin-backed blinds.

Now it was Bromley's turn for its OMO routes to drop their upper deck; LSs were available and that was that, so the 61 lost its DMSs on 30 September, followed by the 126 and 138 on 21 October. Aldenham-produced temporary blinds were also in evidence here, though the intended blinds did arrive in time (and differed through being of a Gill Sans bold-derived font). On 6 October the LS routes terminating in or staging through Staines could find themselves enjoying the amenities of the brand new Staines Bus Station. On 24 November the S2 at Dalston and S3 at West Ham were converted from SMS to LS operation, and the final DMS-to-LS demotion of 1979 took in Holloway's 239 on 3 December.

On 1 October 1979 London Transport's bus arm was separated operationally into eight Districts, which identities were impressed on the public by means of a sticker on the nearside applied by the end of the year.

THE LONDON LS

Left: **LS 354 (AYR 354T) was allocated to West Ham for the conversion of the S3 from SMS on 24 November 1979. In this September 1980 shot it's only going as far as Stratford, though the S3 was very short to begin with. Half a lifetime later, LS 354 could be seen at Harrow Weald in the red and cream livery of Harrow Buses (see page 102).**
Haydn Davies

The final arrivals of the 1979 order were used to alleviate breakdown-related shortages of BLs on the 247 and 247B at North Street, taking over on 5 January 1980, and that was it as far as new LSs were concerned; for the time being, at any rate. Quiet descended over the class; repaints ambled along at two or three per month and eventually, in August, LS 1 emerged from overhaul, in time to prompt the other members of the first batch of six to start going into Aldenham. Hounslow had taken a liking to this bus, however, and enthusiastic staff added a black skirt and grey roof pod to it while keeping the chrome fittings highly polished. Five of the first six had been outshopped by the end of 1980 and LS 5 followed in January 1981. On 10 May Turnham Green was closed, and among its other routes, the E3 migrated with its nine LSs to the new Stamford Brook. The new garage inherited its predecessor's code of V.

Below: **Where east London shades off into Essex, LS 413 (BYW 413V) of North Street is seen during a bright day in April 1980. The 247 and 247B were the last routes to receive new LSs of the original specification, even if they didn't last that long on these particular routes.**
Haydn Davies

Above: **The 90 received Metrobuses on 27 September 1980. LS 138 (THX 138S), seen in April, was transferred to Uxbridge to start LSs off there.** *Haydn Davies*

Below: **LS 219 (THX 219S) came from Hanwell to Uxbridge in January 1981, and is seen later that year on the outskirts of that far-flung suburb.** *Haydn Davies*

From July 1981, examples of the LS 7-57 batch started going in for overhaul, followed by autumn by LSs from the next batch. Progress was to prove very slow, with outshopping not evident until December and not really getting going in earnest until the following spring.

On 21 June 1980 the S3 was extended from Hackney Central to Stoke Newington, adding just LS 435 on transfer from Holloway to furnish this alteration, but changes in 1980 were few. As part of the otherwise extensive 27 September programme the S3 was withdrawn between Stratford and Maryland, while Fulwell's 90 was converted to M operation, causing the despatch of the LSs to Uxbridge to begin the conversion from SMS of the 98 and 204.

From time to time the old red-green connection would endure when London Transport helped out Green Line, and on 10 August Cricklewood's LS 108 did one journey on the 734 to fill in for a disabled Volvo coach (DV 2). LS 66 out of Elmers End was less lucky when on 11 August it ploughed into a house along the 289's line of route. The pay agreement with the union that permitted the use of any appropriate vehicles on OMO routes (and that gave rise to the conversion of DMs to dual-purpose Ds) applied to LSs as well; at North Street two LSs (412 and 413) from the 247 and 247B were beginning to wander to the 103

and 294, covering for Titans suffering teething problems and equipped for this purpose with blind panels adapted from ultimate panels out of the now-departed DMSs, while at Harrow Weald, farebox-equipped LS 245 from the H1 was sighted on other routes from that garage. By the end of the year Loughton was putting LSs out regularly on the 167.

With the conversions of Uxbridge's SMS routes to LS (helped during November by the input of spare examples from five garages, though LS 148 needed to be repaired after being stolen from the garage and crashed) and the sweep of Ms into Edgware at the end of 1980, all normal service Swifts were now gone, leaving just those supporting the long-established MBAs on the Red Arrow services out of three garages. During 1980 London Transport inspected two National 2s of the revised design, with the radiator now moved to the front to accommodate Leyland's O.680 engine. WRN 413V, owned by Leyland but operated by Fishwick, was examined between April and May, but it was not until October, when Ribble's DBV 841W was inspected, that a solid order was placed, and this would be for 69, numbered LS 438-506. From having come late to the type, London Transport was about to employ the second largest fleet of Leyland Nationals in operation.

CHAPTER FIVE

THE RED ARROW NATIONAL 2s

The first of the Red Arrow-bound National 2s, LS 438, made an appearance at Chiswick at the end of 1980 but returned to British Leyland's facility at Apsley, Nottingham without being taken into stock. Deliveries of the 69 National 2s duly commenced in February, but the need to return some to Nottingham (where pre-service checks and fitting out took place) for modifications caused the planned entry into service on routes 500 and 507, scheduled to be treated first, to be put back from 29 March with the 502 and 513 taking their place in the order of introduction. Capacity was B24D+46.

They had LT's specified ribbed Treadmaster flooring in the standee area and fareboxes were fitted. Although the fan was deleted, the classic roof pod remained, and at the rear there were now four-piece rear lights. To train drivers in advance of their arrival, LSs 6, 7 and 300 were drafted into Victoria.

The completion of Uxbridge's rout of SMSs was achieved by converting Hanwell's E3 from LS to M at the same time the E1 and E2 exchanged their DMSs for Metrobuses; the low bridge that had prohibited DMSs on the E3 was not an obstacle to Ms, which were slightly

Below: **The 230 was converted from RM to LS OMO on 31 January 1981. LS 297 (YYE 297T) was already based at Leyton, having been there since new in March 1979, and in August 1981 is seen at Whipps Cross roundabout.** *Haydn Davies*

lower in height. Industrial difficulty, however, dragged the E3's completion out until June from its official 17 January 1981 commencement date. Before they left Hanwell, the E3's LSs had turned out from time to time on the E1 and E2, while other regular wanderings now included the 271 at Holloway and 194 at Elmers End.

Extensive changes to routes in the Hackney and Walthamstow area on 31 January saw the 235 split in two, the main route now terminating at Leytonstone and the northern section becoming new route 206. With the concurrent conversion of Leyton's 55 from DMS to RM operation, the garage now lacked double-deck OMO buses and the N96 had to be converted to LS operation, indeed the first scheduled Nationals on a night route. Stock was provided for these by the OMO conversion of the 230 with LSs. Together with transfers from North Street and Hornchurch after the conversion to T of the 247B and 248A, the existing balance of work at Leyton was maintained.

The 194 at Elmers End was seeing so much LS operation alongside its official DMSs that the Sunday service was designated officially converted to LS on 22 February. Another extensive route change programme bowed on 25 April, and one of its tenets was the most useful extension of the 111 from Cranford to Heathrow Airport. Three LSs were transferred into Hounslow; one ex-Holloway and two from Uxbridge. The most important aspect, however, was where premises were concerned; over the last few years London Transport had embarked upon the construction of fully-appointed new garages, and it was time for the largest of these,

Ash Grove, to open. On 25 April it took on the allocations of both Dalston and Hackney, which were closed, and one of Dalston's routes thus to go in was the 236. The S2, ejected from Dalston, did not pass to Ash Grove but to Poplar (adding an extension in service to its new base from Bromley-by-Bow), thus releasing the 173 from Poplar to West Ham and the S3 into Ash Grove. The LSs into the new garage weren't the only ones, as the National 2s had now arrived, and after storage at variously, British Leyland's Nottingham premises and, once in London, Bow, Clapton and Poplar, were ready for service. Dalston drivers were trained on them before transferring to Ash Grove. Accordingly, on 25 April the 502 came in en bloc from Hackney, together with the Victoria allocation of the 513, and both used LSs from the outset. Neither Merlins nor Swifts operated from the new garage, and by July they were all gone, because between 9 and 23 May Victoria treated the 500 and 507 to LSs and Walworth did the 501 between 8-18 June. Even the rather novelty 639 joined the ranks of National 2 operators, officially on 22 June and operated most often by LS 473.

Stamford Brook's LSs left the E3 by 21 May, with the release of enough Ms to take over their pitch finally. The LSs were apportioned out between various garages, as there were more than a handful of the class needing attention for one reason or another; one ongoing perceived problem was a throttle surge blamed for the two most major accidents since service entry. To address this, examples had their fuel pumps remounted at Turnham Green, the former

Above: **West Ham LSs 307 (AYR 307T) and 305 (AYR 305T) display either end of the 173's extent as they pose at Becontree Heath on a sunny day in August 1981, four months after the 173 was reallocated from Poplar to West Ham.** *Haydn Davies*

Right: **1981 was the year of the National 2 in London, with 69 delivered to take over the Red Arrow routes and see off the last Merlins and Swifts. The vehicles themselves were an attractive update of the original, with the front-mounted radiator adding overall length. The sound of them alone announced their appearance even before you saw them! On 19 May 1981 LS 490 (GUW 490W), new to Victoria, arrives at the 500's Victoria terminus.** *John Laker*

garage which had been set aside since closure for minor modifications of this nature. On 27 May Hounslow lent Harrow Weald LSs 2, 51, 53 and 54 to serve as extras on the 209 on the occasion of the Pinner Fair. At Uxbridge, appearances of LSs on the 222 and 223 during the summer were tempered by the reverse visits of Ms to the 204.

The 194's Sunday flirtation with LSs was put to an end on 14 June and appearances of the type in lieu of DMSs tightened up thereafter, following a Market Assessment Programme undertaken at East Croydon station. On 20 July the S2 was given a weekdays extension taking it round a circle from its normal Kenninghall Roundabout stand at Clapton. On 25 July,

Above: **Three years after the entry into service of LS 443 (GUW 443W), seen approaching Victoria in May 1984, the flat fare on the 507 has risen from 20p to 30p, but no physical changes have otherwise yet taken place.** *Haydn Davies*

Left: **Victoria's new LSs were also put to use on the 639, a short and short-lived service linking King's Cross with the Vale Royal Estate. A blind out of an SMS has been repurposed, though it doesn't quite fit. Nobody's aboard LS 473 (GUW 473W) anyway, and the route would be withdrawn on 24 September 1981.** *Haydn Davies*

Above: **There have been six London bus routes numbered 255, and this one was the second, existing between 31 March 1979 and 4 September 1982. Only one Loughton LS was needed to serve the generally quiet Roding Valley corridor that had previously been the preserve of the 254, and on this August 1981 day LS 194 (THX 194S) was it. After overhaul, this bus would go on to rather greater things (see page 40).** *Haydn Davies*

however, a change featuring LSs was executed which would underscore the progressive drawing back of London Transport behind its politically-defined administrative borders in the next two years or so. This was the 247, which despite being the longest route in London at an eye-watering 24 miles in length, was withdrawn completely, with only cursory amendments to neighbouring routes; London Country, with much reduced Essex County Council subsidy,

was expected to fill in in its absence. In the same general Essex-borders sector, the 250 and 255 were combined in operation with complicated one-way loops on each before and after Loughton Station; in any case, the 250's Limes Farm projections were withdrawn. Two days later, the 246 at Hornchurch was converted from T to LS operation, using six of the former North Street LSs made spare by the withdrawal of the 247.

Right: **During the late 1970s and early 1980s Hornchurch garage had to juggle its proportion of Titans and LSs, dependent on which route the planners decided needed to go under Cranham station bridge more. The change to the 246 that projected it in that direction was facilitated by the conversion of the route from T to LS on 27 July 1981. LS 130 (THX 130S), based at Hornchurch since new, is seen at Noak Hill.** *Haydn Davies*

Above: **New route 256 was introduced on 28 November 1981 to bring London Transport operation to the County Park Estate, right against the easternmost border of the GLC. The two LSs needed for it were supplied when the busy 248 was converted to T operation and rerouted away from the low bridge at Cranham station in the process. LS 372 (BYW 372V) of Hornchurch is seen in September 1982.**
Haydn Davies

Hardly much of a going concern with the area north of Kings Cross by no means revitalised, the 639 came off on 26 September. Still, on 25 October the 239 at Holloway regained DMS operation, its LSs passing to Peckham to single-deck the 78 in order to allow that route's current MDs to leave to provide a 100% Metropolitan allocation at the newly-opened Plumstead (PD) garage; that also presaged LS operation on the N85 and N86. At Norbiton, the 218 and 219 each received a peak-hours extension beyond Kingston to Ham, Beaufort Road.

Finally for 1981, and returning to Essex, some Hornchurch-based routes swapped their single- and double-deckers on 28 November in order to forestall the threat of Cranham station bridge. Thus did the 248A have to take on a single LS when a morning schoolday journey was extended round a loop to and from its regular Upminster station terminus. Having been withdrawn between Cranham and Upminster Station via St Mary's Lane, where the offending bridge was located, the 248 could now assume T operation, exchanging its LSs with the 252 instead. On Sundays, the previous arrangements still applied. To complete the set, Hornchurch LSs inaugurated a new route 256 between Romford and County Park Estate.

Other than minor rerouteings to the 111, 206 and 502 in January, 1982's programme where LSs were concerned did not get going until 30 January, when the appearances of Ms on Muswell Hill's 244 on Saturdays were formalised. The 248A was amended on 8 March to remove the journey that passed under St Mary's Lane, and Ts could now appear again with impunity. From 17 April the 234A at Croydon started receiving LSs to replace its BLs, but not enough of them could be made available until June, and its last BL came off only after the extensive service changes of 4 September. Over the first half of the year LSs would visit Norbiton's 211.

The main event of 1981, politically, had been the institution of the Labour-run GLC's Fares Fair policy and its subsequent overturning in the High Court. Reductions were coming, to reflect the sharp drop in custom since fares had to be doubled on 21 March 1982, but the LSs as a class were only obliquely affected. Still, further retrenchment applied to the London borders when neighbouring councils could not be persuaded to fund cross-border services, and those into Essex were set to suffer first. On 24 April this process commenced through the gutting of a number of Loughton's

Right: **The LS gained ascendance at Loughton when all three of its double-deck routes were unceremoniously stripped of their Titans on 4 September 1982. The 20A had already been gutted to comply with the reduction of subsidy by Essex County Council to this border-crossing service, and by the time LS 133 (THX 133S) was seen in September was going no further south than Loughton Station, bar some school journeys to West Hatch School in Chigwell.** *Haydn Davies*

Right: **Loughton lost the 255 on 4 September 1982, but to take its place as the 250's offshoot was new route 250A, serving its other end out of Waltham Cross and linking it with Upshire in replacement of the 217B's journeys to this point. LS 89 (OJD 889R), newly transferred from Peckham, is seen in the first month of the new order.** *Haydn Davies*

Right: **The 78 regained double-deckers with the 4 September 1982 changes, but this time the LSs were replaced by Titans. Curiously, for such a premier structure, Tower Bridge has always had a rather vestigial bus service, as the points immediately to the south of the bridge are where no tourists would want to go. Peckham's LS 398 (BYW 398V), seen in August with its foglights missing, was transferred to Loughton.** *Haydn Davies*

services. Although the 206 lost its evening and Sunday service beyond Leytonstone Station to Walthamstow Central, the addition of a daily Loughton allocation to fill some of the gaps lost by the hacking of the 20A obliged garage projections from Grange Farm. However, trouble with clearing all this with staff members tasked with fitting blinds and ferrying buses (this work done on overtime) meant that Loughton didn't commence until 16 May, and since Leyton's Sunday allocation had come off with the main changes, there was no service on Sunday until that date. To bridge the 20A's loss from the south, the 235 was extended from Leytonstone Station to Woodford Wells. At Hornchurch, the 252 was now able to regain full T operation, though a local dispute postponed this in practice until mid-May.

Elsewhere in town, Muswell Hill's 244 was withdrawn entirely, the duties lost being recouped by taking Holloway's share of the 210 off, while at Hounslow, the 116 lost its roads beyond Hounslow to Brentford and the S2 was pulled back again to Clapton, Kenninghall Road.

At least 1982 was a banner year for LS overhauls, with examples from all Mark I batches going through works; at the start of the year LS 12 had been examined at Aldenham to check how a sample vehicle was doing one month after outshopping and the results pronounced satisfactory. Three long-term disused LSs were gradually repaired during the year and returned to service, while LS 16 was sent to Merton in July to train drivers awaiting a large influx of the class there.

The mammoth set of changes that reduced LT's service roster by 13% was postponed once to address the sheer impact it would have, but finally introduced on 4 September and affected the LS class no less than any other. Perhaps the most significant of these changes was the complete demotion of Loughton to LS operation, taking the only recently introduced Titans off routes 20, 167 and what remained of the 20A. Many of the Nationals needed were transferred from Peckham's 78 (and N85 and N86 at night), which got an upper deck back with the introduction of Titans. To add capacity to Loughton, whose PVR was by now small enough to beg questions of unviability, the Leyton allocation was taken off the 206. The 250/255 pair was altered by withdrawing the latter, while a new 250A was introduced to fill the gap left by the withdrawal of the 217 between Waltham Cross and Upshire. At Hornchurch, the 244 number was revived after four months to identify a new Romford-Upminster Park Estate service and the 246 gained a limited Sunday service. All LS operation left the 248 (LSs having endured on Sundays) and 248A (now fully converted to Titans). The 244 and 246 were intended to interwork and blinds were produced that carried the third number of each for ease of winding, but agreement to twin the routes wasn't forthcoming.

At West Ham, the diversion of route 278 to Stoke Newington rather than to Walthamstow replaced the S3 in its entirely but also obliged its conversion from T (and holdout DMSs) to LS owing to the low bridges to be found along those roads. Leyton's 230 lost its entire evening

Left: **The 246 wended its way around Romford rather than going into that town, but on 4 September 1982 it gained a new partner that did just that. It was known as 244, and the joint operation was made easier (if not more aesthetically pleasing) by adding the third number on the destination blind so as to reduce the driver's need to keep winding the third track. LS 121 (THX 121S) came out of overhaul to Hornchurch in March 1983, and is still looking smart six months later.** *Haydn Davies*

service to make up for being extended otherwise from Whipps Cross to Leytonstone. The 236 at Ash Grove was cut between Finsbury Park and Stroud Green, breaking a longstanding link across Finsbury Park.

To the west and south-west, Uxbridge's 98 added Ms to help out on two school journeys before this role was altered in December to accommodate an extra pair of LSs. Hounslow's 111 was converted from LS to M, while Merton's DMS routes 127, 152 and 189 were all converted from DMS to LS, introducing the class at that garage; the 57 also had to take a proportion of LSs on Saturdays. The 215 was converted from BL to LS operation and by necessity reallocated from Kingston to Norbiton, and at the same time as converting the 71's vestigial Sunday OMO service from BL to LS, Norbiton gained another LS service with the simultaneous conversion from BL of the 216. Its Staines, Wraysbury Road projections and those of the 218 and 219 beyond Kingston to Ham came off, similar economies being made throughout the network by snipping away at evening and Sunday services; to this end Elmers End's 12A lost most of its duties between South Croydon, Swan and Sugar Loaf and South Croydon Garage. Bromley's 146 gained LSs to replace its BLs, underscoring the progressive sidelining of the Bristol LHs as the larger-capacity LSs became available.

In town, the Red Arrow routes found themselves only superficially altered, with the Trafalgar Square leg of the 500 taken off and the 513 losing its evening service, but twelve LSs were made redundant and delicensed. Finally, accompanying the structural upheaval were changes to fare collection methods, the only such accruing to LSs on 4 September being the conversion of the H1 and S2 from farebox flat-fare to the regular graduated-fare system.

After the turmoil of 4 September, changes for the rest of 1982 were few, and both were at Loughton. On 1 November one journey in each peak of the 206's peak-hour projections to Loughton garage were rerouted to serve Debden and extended to Loughton Station. On 4 December it was recognised just how unviable the remnants of the 20A were by reconfiguring it as 201, operating from Ongar to Epping (Loughton during daytimes and on to Buckhurst Hill on Sundays).

A thought to technological progression saw Norbiton's LS 268 fitted with a dot-matrix blind display during May 1982. One line deep, it showed route number on the offside and destination on the nearside, the latter feature of which would recycle to two intermediate points every five seconds.

One further Leyland National joined LT's fleet in 1982, but wouldn't find itself going into stage service; former Plymouth 22 (SCO 422L) was acquired from Brakell on 13 May and given the service bus identity 1234L. A direct replacement for Swift SPB 753, it would serve the next six years as a publicity bus and shop.

After the wave of retrenchments across the Essex border, it was time to similarly treat routes going into Surrey; while those pushing south from Sutton had been pulled back at the same time as changes to Loughton, LSs factored into a set of changes implemented on 29 January 1983. The highest-profile casualty was the 219, which was withdrawn completely. Redressing the balance at Norbiton was an extension of the 216 from Kingston to Tolworth over the 211, which was also withdrawn, and a particularly ambitious addition of a Norbiton LS allocation to the 72, incorporating live garage journeys from Tolworth Broadway. Joint

Above: **During 1982 LS 268 (YYE 268T) was fitted with a dot-matrix blind box that promised to make redundant the expensive and cumbersome linen blinds of long-established tradition, but it could only display one line of information. When seen loading up in Kingston garage in June 1982 it is on the 219, soon to be withdrawn; wait five seconds and the route's major via point will be shown.** *Haydn Davies*

Left: **So many buses were made spare after the losses at Norbiton that it was decided to fill the gap with something as local as could be found, even if it terminated as far away as Tolworth. That was the 72, normally operated by Shepherd's Bush with DMSs. The input of two-thirds of it into Norbiton used up the LSs and prompted an extension in service to Kingston. Here at Eden Street during August 1983 is LS 186 (THX 186S), carrying white-on-black numberplates.** *Tony Wilson*

working was applied to two pairs of LS routes interconnecting at Staines, taking in the 116 and 203 as well as the 216 and 218, but cross-border frequencies on all of them were reduced. Norbiton's LSs could now pop up on the 85 and 131 now that blinds covering all the garage's routes were fitted.

Also on 29 January came the first post-Red Arrow employment of National 2s when the P4

at Stockwell was expanded with an extension to Lewisham that could now employ larger buses than its previous BLs. A proposal to reallocate it to Peckham had been cancelled and the introduction of LSs had slipped from the previous year due to stand issues at Brockley which were addressed by extending the route to Lewisham. The vehicles in question were LSs 483-486, 488 and 489 and were upseated

to B36D, for which they were recoded 3LS3/1. Curiously, flat fares remained on its original section to Brockley Rise but switched to conventional fares beyond there to Lewisham; otherwise the P3 and P5 had discarded farebox operation with effect from a week earlier. The P5, additionally, was taken off Rotherhithe Street in the peninsula from 9 April and rerouted along the main Salter Road. Finally,

on 22 May, to accompany the 'Just The Ticket' fares revision (which thankfully, reduced most of them this time!), farebox operation throughout the network was discontinued for good. On 26 February the 97A had a Leyton allocation added, introducing LSs alongside the Walthamstow Titans.

Since 4 September 1982 a double-decker had had to stand in for an LS on Uxbridge's route

Above: **Three buses in a single place on one route may be a boon for the photographer, but it surely means that timekeeping has gone wrong and that somewhere else down the line, passengers are waiting longer than they should. Accordingly, the middle bus of this trio at Brent Cross in April 1983 will be going no further than Archway, so as to fill the gap made earlier. The buses are Muswell Hill-allocated LSs 170 (THX 170S), 197 (THX 197S) and 310 (AYR 310T).** *Haydn Davies*

Left: **Following their introduction to Uxbridge, LSs had turned out on the 224, otherwise the province of Metrobuses. LS 437 (BYW 437V), the last of the London Transport Mark Is and based at Uxbridge since October 1980, is seen in November 1981.** *Haydn Davies*

Right: **April 1983 sees Hounslow's LS 131 (THX 131S) pulling into Heathrow Central bus station in lieu of a Metrobus, which type had otherwise taken over the 111. It would remain at Hounslow until 1991.**
Haydn Davies

98 (an M) and Merton's 152 (a DMS) during schooldays, but the 29 January 1983 changes brought timetable revisions that enabled these routes to assume their intended full LS operation. LSs continued to stand in for Ms on the otherwise recently converted 111 and 202 (the latter seeing them predominantly from May), Uxbridge's 222 and 224 (and the 98, still) and Hornchurch's 248 and 248A as well as the familiar berth for rogue LSs, Elmers End's 194 (which was joined by the summer by tentative appearances on the 54. Ms at Hounslow returned the favour on the 116, 117, 203 and 257. By March new blinds had been fitted to Croydon's LSs, allowing appearances on the 166, 166A and 234, and at West Ham LSs

occasionally revisited the S1 as well as popping up on the 262 with masked blinds from the 278.

On 23 April a set of alterations to long-established routes in the Harrow area transposed the eastern ends of the 114 and 140; the former now terminated at Mill Hill Broadway with the odd projection to Mill Hill East Station. It had pretty much outgrown its LSs by now, and Ms from the 140's allocation put in at the same time started appearing, but never enough to threaten the Nationals' dominance at Harrow Weald. On the same day the 182's Sunday-only Harrow Weald allocation was replaced by an increase at Alperton. Reflecting what would become a series of partial conversions as Harrow Weald figured out how best to utilise

Right: **Only seven months after its introduction, Bromley's 261 was converted to OMO on 23 April 1983 and had to make do with LSs, due to the garage not being familiar with the Titans otherwise entering service in Selkent District. LS 272 (YYE 272T) had come out of overhaul to Bromley in February 1983 and is seen that August at Lewisham bus station with another one queueing behind it.**
Haydn Davies

Above and below: **LS 402 (BYW 402V) was Harrow Weald's elegant answer to the call by LT to customise buses for the 50th anniversary of the organisation. In September 1983 it is seen along the 136 road.** *Both: Haydn Davies*

unveiled a second showbus, LS 402. On this bus the window surrounds were in gold, and it was kept on the 136 (usually on peak-hour running number HD43). The absolute pinnacle of aesthetics on the otherwise humble Leyland National in London Transport came when LS 194 was unveiled at the Chiswick Gala on 2 July in full 'General' livery, complete with enormous embossed 'LEYLAND' lettering on the front. Only the roof differed from the other 1933-liveried buses due to its being white rather than silver, but the effect was spectacular. As Croydon's pet, it stuck fast to the 234A, with the odd foray to the 234. Later in the year the effect was topped off with the addition of blinds in Johnston font, a feature which would spread slowly fleetwide over the next few years. By August, in time for the Aldenham Spectacular open day on 25 September, came two more showbus LSs; LS 200, outshopped to Loughton, had the garage name added in red across the roundel bar plus a thin white band below the windows, and rather more ornately, LS 438 at Ash Grove was repainted with a white roof and even given a name; *City Belle*.

LSs continued to help out stricken Green Line workings, but by now this work had fallen to Red Arrow National 2s out of Victoria; on 12 July LS 482 did the honours on a 717 and on the 25th another stood in for a 730.

On 29 May the 235's recently-introduced projections to Woodford Wells were taken off in late evenings due to blockage of the route by parked cars, but at the same time of day from 25 June the 117 was projected from Hounslow to Brentford. A rerouteing of the P4 in Brockley on the same day now took it via the hitherto unserved Brockley Grove. The 216's enlargement in January had proven a bit too much to handle in one go, so from 11 July operation was sectionalised across Kingston. In the fast revitalising Beckton area, a new Asda superstore had now been run up as the focal point of the area and the 173 was diverted off Newham Way to serve it, beginning on 10 September.

New Ms into Fulwell released enough earlier examples to put into Norbiton from 29 October to begin easing its LSs off the 72, but on the same day a severe change to the 189 turned it from a fairly useful (if loss-making) outer-suburban link into a stump that would struggle for survival thereafter; in spite of now commencing from Brixton rather than Clapham Common, it was curtailed at Tooting Mitre. Night Buses were growing too, and for our purposes the N96, still the only LS-operated night route, was one of several to have a Saturday night service added. The LSs released from Norbiton formed top-ups at six garages.

Below: **LS 146 (THX 146S), transferred from West Ham to Poplar in October 1984, looks smart with a black bumper, even though that wasn't part of the original paint specification. It is seen in November 1984 at the Lea (or Lee) Valley Ice Centre on the S2's extension to that point.**
Haydn Davies

Left: **There's a big queue of buses round the back of Uxbridge garage on 20 November 1983; two of the five Nationals identifiable alongside three Metrobuses are LSs 219 (THX 219S) and 209 (THX 209S).** *John Laker*

their Ms for capacity increases over LSs, the 114 was actually officially converted to Ms on Sundays on 19 June but this only lasted two weeks due to turning difficulties at the garage. Eventually Harrow Weald's LSs began to make appearances on the 140 as well.

The 4 September 1982 changes had introduced several RM routes that were felt perfect for one-manning; one of these had been the 261, operated by Bromley, but when OMO came on 23 April the garage still had no OMO double-decks and it was not planned to put any in, so LSs had to do and were immediately overwhelmed.

1983 was London Transport's Golden Jubilee year, and vehicles of myriad types from all over the system were treated to cream or even gold relief bands and gold leaf transfers to celebrate LT's fiftieth anniversary. Harrow Weald had led the way in terms of the LS, with LS 382 semi-customised at the end of 1982 with a gold fleetname, and in April it

Below: **Hounslow's LS 157 (THX 157S) has a little further to go on the 117 when sighted outside its home garage during April 1983. Once its relief driver turns up and plugs in his Almex E, the bus can be on its way again.** *Haydn Davies*

This picture: **The treatment afforded to Croydon's LS 194 (THX 194S) for LT's Golden Jubilee was truly splendid. The Serck numberplates are also worth noting, as no other LSs were known to have worn them during the type's time.** *Haydn Davies*

Below: **LS 438** *City Belle* **(GUW 438W) was the Red Arrow fleet's Golden Jubilee representative, seen at Waterloo on 17 October 1983.** *John Laker*

Left: **At the end of 1983 two Red Arrow LSs were allocated to West Ham and one more to Poplar. The appearance of LS 448 (GUW 448W) on the 173 is thus most unusual.**
Haydn Davies

Until now original Nationals and their National 2 developments had never been used on one another's routes, but sometimes shortages obliged the unthinkable, and in September LSs 447 and 448, spare from the reductions to Red Arrow services, were fitted with Almex baseplates and licensed at West Ham (working on the 173, but very occasionally also the 262 and S1) and LS 459 similarly at Poplar. No alteration was made to their seating,

no doubt nonplussing boarders who expected there to be many more seats! Adding to the variety at West Ham, all that garage's LSs were going round with black bumpers. Between January and March 1984 LSs 503 and 504 were in use at Bromley, but these unorthodox National 2 wanderings were frowned upon and plans set in train to concentrate the surplus in one place, namely the 210; this wouldn't actually come to pass for two more years.

Below: **The third unusual deployment of National 2s over the cusp of 1983-84 took LSs 503 and 504 to Bromley. Here they are in their temporary home garage on 4 February 1984, alongside normally-allocated LSs 46 and 370 .**
R. C. Riley

CHAPTER SIX

FROM LT TO LBL

Two days into the New Year that saw LT become LRT came a minor revision of the division structure which deleted Tower and Watling Districts. On 3 January 1984 came a new venture that combined the traditional foresight into planning for newly-developed areas with an innovative twist in aesthetic terms. This was the D1, or Docklands Clipper, set going with six overhauled LSs (53, 165, 171, 260, 267 and 326) painted into an attractive dedicated livery of red with white band and stripes and allocated to Poplar. It added service to areas of the Isle of Dogs not otherwise reached

via the perimeter-using routes 277 or 56, and although a couple of rerouteings intermediately and at the terminus had to be implemented temporarily not long after introduction, it proved a keeper. The allocation of National 2s to East End garages was thought to have been in preparation for this, but the three buses in question were returned to store by the spring. There would be other opportunities for the type at non-Red Arrow garages before much more time had passed. LS 7 was fitted with D1 blinds to serve as a spare, while the liveried ones were apt to pop up on the 108 and S2.

Below: **The D1's livery was splendid and really flattered the six LSs that came out of overhaul to receive it. But in this November 1984 shot, there's nothing for Poplar's LS 171 (THX 171S) to serve - no buildings or infrastructure at all yet!**
Haydn Davies

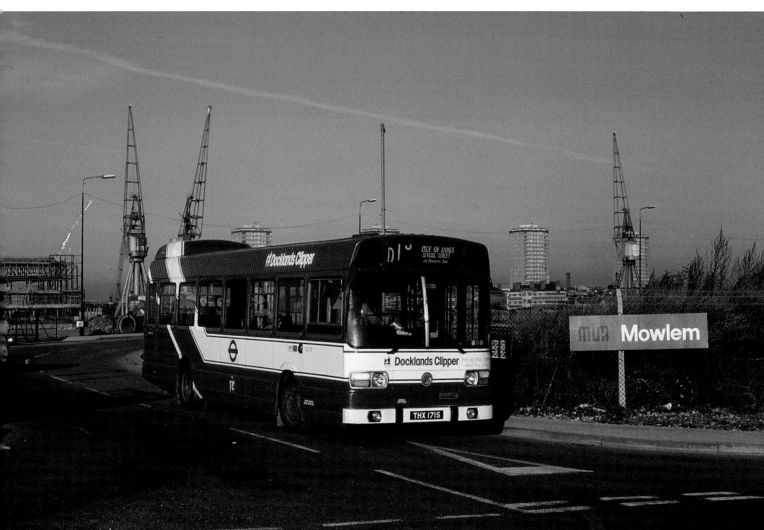

The closure of Kingston garage on 14 January, amongst other changes, caused the conversion from LS to M of the two-bus Sunday service on the 71. On 4 February came the major round of changes in the same area and further to the east; the Norbiton share of the 72 was withdrawn without having finished its upgrading from LS to M, and at Croydon the 234A was withdrawn, prompting an extension of the 12A from Selsdon via Purley to Old Lodge Lane to cover part of it. LS 194 was returned to red at this point, though the large 'LEYLAND' lettering on the front remained and gold fleetnumbers were applied again; it worked on the last journey of the 234A and, with no further need for LSs at Croydon, was transferred to Merton (LS 231 was late out, not going until twelve days after the official conversion). The 127 was converted from LS back to DMS upon its reallocation from Merton to Croydon and similar extension over the middle part of the 234A, and finally the 117's Sunday service to Brentford was withdrawn, though it did receive bifurcations off the main route to Ashford Hospital during visiting hours.

Despite the repaint of LS 194, the other two Jubilee showbuses (Loughton's LS 200 and Harrow Weald's LS 402) were subtle enough to stay under the radar, and the latter remained in its special livery until April 1986. However, the source of their improvement now started coming under threat. Under orders to cut the costs of overhauling or risk Aldenham's closure, LT investigated putting the work out to tender; LSs were included as well as DMSs, Ms and Ts, and on 22 December 1983 Midland Red took three LSs (124, 159 and 216), returning them on 27 February 1984. Over the first three months of 1984 LSs 34, 163, 177 and 277 were sent to ECW at Lowestoft for body attention, with all mechanical work done by Leyland at Nottingham. The first LS to find itself struck off fleet strength, however, was LS 185, damaged in a rear-end accident in June 1983; its seats were donated to Mark 2 LS 464 and its front replaced that of LS 384. The remains officially left stock in October 1986. The tail end of the contract overhauls took rather longer to return than envisaged, LSs 195 and 340 not coming back till October; this and the unsatisfactory quality of work done by contrast with Aldenham soured LT on the concept and indeed concerted effort was put in to streamline Aldenham's operations so that the same volume of work could be done with 60% of the previous staff. Only two LSs numbered below LS 300 (plus LS 185) had not been overhauled by the end of 1984, and those two (the oldest straggler being LS 31) were taken in during December.

Uxbridge's LS routes 98 (on weekdays) and 224 (on Saturdays) began receiving limited support by Ms when a handful of the new double-deckers found themselves allocated to the garage, and Harrow Weald was helped out in a similar fashion on 8 March, routes 114, 136, 209 and 258 all featuring. Extensive expansion of Night Bus services on the night of 13/14 April saw the sole LS-operated N96 projected at either end, to Chingford Station in the north and to Trafalgar Square in the centre. The day saw the introduction of a summer-Sunday extension of the 116 beyond Staines to Thorpe Park, its last day being 9 September.

Stockwell's reseated National 2s added a second route to their quiver on 28 April when new route 115 was introduced to give Bedford Hill a first-time bus service. The additional complement was made up of upseated LS 464, joined a little later by similarly-treated LSs 459 and 491. More important was the projection of Peckham's P3 to London Bridge via unserved roads that would soon become tremendously busy. As well as taking on LS 226 on loan

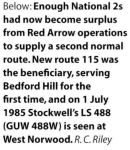

Below: **Enough National 2s had now become surplus from Red Arrow operations to supply a second normal route. New route 115 was the beneficiary, serving Bedford Hill for the first time, and on 1 July 1985 Stockwell's LS 488 (GUW 488W) is seen at West Norwood.** *R. C. Riley*

Left: **The P4's and now the 115's fleet of LSs soon began to wander to the 170, adding an unexpected comparison with the four new experimental types appearing in service on that route at spaced intervals. LS 491 (GUW 491W) crosses Trafalgar Square in September 1984.**
Haydn Davies

from Elmers End to account for breakdowns to its National 2s, plus the odd example from Peckham, Stockwell had now received blind sets including the 170, so that LSs could turn out on that increasingly eclectic route and thus unwittingly provide even further comparison with the growing number of experimentals that made it their home. Similar anomalies during the year were the spread of Norbiton LSs to all of 85, 131 and 213, plus visits by Uxbridge LSs to the 128 and 222 and of Harrow Weald LSs to the 140. Victoria National 2s filled in regularly for stricken Green Line vehicles, with forays reported to routes 714, 715, 770 and 798. Not a strange working but a livery anomaly was the appearance of red entrance doors on Peckham's LS 263 and Uxbridge's LS 15, while the bumpers on Peckham's LS 276, front and back, were red.

Below: **Norbiton was in the habit of putting out its LSs on M-operated routes 85 and 131 during 1984; just such a working that October is of LS 300 (AYR 300T) at Kingston.**
Haydn Davies

The route number 254 returned on 12 May and to the Loughton area to boot. This time it was a route 'across the top' from Waltham Cross to Epping. Loughton also saw its 206 given a summer-Sunday extension from Claybury Hospital to Epping (which lasted until 27 October) and the return of its evening service into Walthamstow. Much further to the south, Bromley's LSs commenced a new one-bus service numbered 284 which linked Orpington Station and Petts Wood via hitherto unserved Poverest Road. 'Strawberry-pickers'

special' blinds appeared on 261s that summer, the affected passengers disembarking at Farnborough for this task.

14 May saw a new Red Arrow route, or rather 'Stationlink' with the shadow route number 555. Operated by Ash Grove's National 2s, it made the circuit of all the main-line stations daily (except for Monday to Friday peak hours), with a companion 'Airlink' (referred to internally as 556) that connected to the last train from Birmingham to Euston to take its passengers onward to the airport. Neither route was meant

to display their internal numbers but did more often than not. The 513 was simultaneously withdrawn during the peak hours and in the evenings. On 1 September the 501 northbound was taken out of the Strand tunnel between the peaks to serve stops in Aldwych.

On 8 August 1984 Bromley's LS 379 suffered fire damage while working TB41 on the 261; it was coming due for overhaul as it was, so the damage was repaired at Aldenham.

Tendering was now imminent, and of the first thirteen routes offered out on 10 October,

LS-operated routes 146, 152, 215 and P4 were among them. Only the middle two would be retained. As if foreseeing its own exit from red operation by this means, Hornchurch's 193 started hosting LSs during the autumn.

On 29 September the 252, unofficially reintroducing LSs on Sundays, was extended from South Hornchurch to Hornchurch. At the very end of Titan production examples were now earmarked to take over the 261 at Bromley from LSs, and this began on 5 October. The 61 was set to follow suit from 4 December, but the

supply ran dry too late and indeed there were still not quite enough to provision the 261's increased Saturday PVR which still included an extension to Brockley Rise.

The 27 October programme, among other things, brought an upper deck back to routes 173 and 278, the latter to account for yet another comprehensive rerouteing which now placed it in support of the 86 west of Stratford. Its narrow roads to Stoke Newington were now put under the responsibility of new route 276 with Poplar LSs, using those displaced by West Ham. Another try was made at pushing the S2 beyond its Clapton terminus; this time it was projected at weekends up the Lea Bridge Road to the Lee Valley Ice Centre. To the southeast, the 180's self-contained Lewisham-Lower Sydenham leg was reconfigured as new LS-operated 181, bringing Nationals to Catford for the first time and using the balance of those leaving West Ham. Finally for 1984, the 216's school journeys on its Tolworth section were converted from LS to M on 26 November.

In October LS 459 was upseated prior to deployment to Stockwell, while LS 354 was fitted at Chiswick with an experimental anti-assault screen. One National 2 spare from Red Arrows but not deployed elsewhere so far was LS 454; it was fitted with a Ratcliff wheelchair lift in the centre doorway (retaining 21 seats in the rear section) and in October moved to Leyton. On 27 November it was put into service from this garage, taking disabled passengers in the boroughs of Newham and Tower Hamlets to the Asda stores at Beckton and on the Isle of Dogs on routes 901-910. An attendant was carried to help the wheelchairs on and off.

Over the Christmas period Metrobuses were hastily added to the route 500 complement at Victoria to cover for a fire at Oxford Circus; they carried old MBA/SMS blinds still in stores. LS 438 was repainted back into red during December.

Above: **LS 454 (GUW 454W) was the first wheelchair-accessible London bus. Spare from Red Arrow work, it was fitted with a wheelchair lift in the central doorway and put to work from Leyton on a network of specially-commissioned routes serving portions unreachable by the main body of the fleet. In May 1985 it is seen at Walthamstow Central on the 906, which was blinded as 'Stratford Shopper' to indicate that it was for use by everyone, not just wheelchair users.**
Haydn Davies

1985 began with a hefty programme implemented on 2 February. In the Walthamstow area, the withdrawal of 'round the corner' route 255 obliged a replacement to be mounted by diverting the 97A to Hackney Central; this route was reallocated to Leyton on Saturdays and thus made wholly LS on that day. The similar reallocation from Walthamstow to Leyton of the 97 on Sundays made up for the 275's withdrawal on that day of the week. The 235 was extended in evenings once again from Woodford Green to Woodford Wells (though this lasted only until 31 March due to parked cars obstructing the stand), but the 224 at Uxbridge lost its Sunday service. The 116's annual Thorpe Park extension came on for the

Left: **Thorpe Park, just beyond the GLC border southwest of Staines, was a popular venue during the 1980s and local route 116 was the first of a few local routes to find themselves extended there on summer Sundays. In September 1984, as the season winds down, Hounslow's LS 266 (THX 266S) demonstrates.**
Haydn Davies

summer on 31 March, and on 27 April the N96 was rerouted between Chingford Mount and Chingford via the main drag.

Times were changing, and in no field was the pace more evident than in the mere name of what the operating organisation was to be called. On 1 April 1985 LRT's bus operations were formally separated as LBL (London Buses Ltd), and ten days later the results of the first tenders were announced. Of the thirteen routes put out, six were won by other operators for takeover in the summer of 1985 and three of them (the 81, 146 and P4) were operated by LSs.

Where the existing fleet was concerned, second overhauls were on the cards, with LS 12 going in first during February and other early examples gathering in store in readiness. By April only LSs 335, 337, 344, 345, 349, 367, 382, 416, 420 and 435 had not been overhauled, and all of these had passed through works by the summer. LS 420 lingered, due to needing to be pulled out of storage at AEC to serve as cover at Uxbridge during May, but by June only LSs 382 and 435 remained to be done. These were delicensed in August, but as it happened, Aldenham would overhaul neither of them. Another programme of contract overhauls was instituted, among others three National 2s (LSs 447, 453 and 497) being selected for treatment by British Leyland at Nottingham and coming back after comparatively speedy treatment that merited the sending of nine further National 2s during the year; the work was divided between

Leyland and ECW. Routine Aldenham first overhauls of National 2s followed on seamlessly from the last of the originals. However, LSs 1, 2, 4 and 5 were delicensed in March, followed by LS 6 in April and LS 3 in June. They were the first LSs to depart stock; LSs 2, 4 and 5 were destined for British Airtours and were painted into that undertaking's attractive blue and white livery for airside use, while LS 1 passed to Red Rover and LS 5 to Dolphin International Displays in St Albans. LS 6 left only in 1987.

27 April saw an element of LS operation reintroduced to Peckham's 78, but the main event came as a side-effect of the 119's one-manning at Bromley. Now inefficient on its own, the schedule was combined with the 138 and converted it to T operation. At Elmers End, the 289 was withdrawn between Elmers End Green and Beckenham Junction, while the new Sunday 194A was pencilled in for LSs either upon its introduction or two weeks later, but this did not yet come to pass. Loughton's 254 was withdrawn and the 189 gained back no more than half a mile with a between-peaks projection from Tooting Mitre to Tooting Broadway Station. The 206's summer leg to Epping was activated on this day, and the route diverted away from Hermon Hill at the same time so that the 235 could take over these roads. The 501 was reallocated from Walworth to Ash Grove, taking with it LSs 442, 448, 451, 461, 477, 494, 496-502 and 504-506 and removing Red Arrow workings from the former. The

'556', this LS-operated route having latterly carried its unofficial number more often than not, was withdrawn and, together with the Inter-Station Night Bus, replaced by two new double-deck night services. Finally for 27 April, a night change saw the only LS-operated route, Leyton's N96, rerouted away from Chingford Hatch on its way to and from Chingford Station.

Tachographs had by now been fitted to Leyton's LSs 61, 261, 275 and 454 plus Victoria's LS 473, permitting their use on private-hire work. From 5 May Loughton was the focus of a ticketing experiment which replaced the garage's complement of Almex E machines with new Timtronic units that were capable of printing both the time of boarding and the number of the individual bus. During May LS 356 was fitted for wheelchair operation and LS 396 followed suit in June, the aim being for them to join LS 454 on its Mobility Bus network. In September LS 268 had its dot-matrix blind box removed at Chiswick and conventional LS blinds restored.

On 1 June the summer-Sunday Thorpe Park extensions of the 216 and 218 were put into action (their last day, as well as the concurrent extension of the 116, being 3 November), but it was on 13 July that commenced the biggest changes ever to the way in which London buses were operated. Long identified as structurally inefficient and perennially money-losing, it was no surprise that the 81 had found itself put on the list of the first routes to go out to tender, and

its award to Len Wright Travel-owned London Buslines (with reclaimed DMSs) cost Hounslow one of its major allocations. Eight LSs were delicensed.

By 3 August 1985 enough DMSs had been made available to officially delete the appearance of LSs on Merton's 57 on Saturdays; variety was maintained here through wanderings to the 156. At Peckham, the P5 was withdrawn and its roads added to the 70

Above: **One day in April 1985 at Kingston, Merton has put LS 96 (OJD 896R) out on the 57, perhaps if just because with a snarled first blind box track, this bus wouldn't have been able to manage the 152 or 189.** *Haydn Davies*

Left: **In order to make Titans available for the one-manning of the 48 on 3 August 1985, one route had to make way at Walthamstow, and this was the 275, which was reallocated to Leyton and converted to LS operation. Seen later that month is LS 255 (THX 255S).** *Haydn Davies*

as an extension from Surrey Docks round the peninsula and on to Peckham; not only did the 70 pass to Peckham in order to inherit the LSs but a new counterpart was introduced numbered 70A, which comprised two early journeys from Peckham to Monument via the main roads. Catford's 181 was introduced on Sundays and extended from Lewisham to Surrey Docks to cover the other end of the P5. At Leyton, the OPO conversion of the 48 forced it to move from Leyton to Walthamstow in exchange for the 275, converting the latter to LS operation (using the examples made spare from the 81 at Hounslow) and obliging live garage journeys to its new base; all remaining Walthamstow (and thus Titan) workings on the 97A came off at the same time. The second LS-operated route to pass to the private sector was the P4, which in its move to National Travel South East, a subsidiary of London Country, actually retained Leyland Nationals but in this case they were B-series SNBs. Five National 2s

were put in store, leaving enough at Stockwell for the 115.

LS route number three was lost on 10 August and this was the 146 at Bromley, ceding to a motley collection of minibuses operated by Crystals Coaches of Orpington. Just one LS was delicensed at Bromley, this being LS 80. Even though the retention of half the first tranche of routes by LBL appeared to be 'business as usual' from the outside, buses had to be tachograph-fitted to measure mileage and their Almex ticket machines were replaced by Wayfarers; an example of this was the 215's complement of LSs at Norbiton.

Aldenham's future was still by no means certain, despite the hard work undertaken to compete with the private sector; starting in October, some of the early LSs undergoing second overhauls were subcontracted to Midland Red, Kent Engineering, ECW and British Leyland (adding insult to injury, at the very portion of Aldenham Works that had been leased to Leyland!). On 15 November it was announced that much of the traditional overhaul work was to be made the responsibility of garages from April 1986, with corresponding redundancies at Aldenham. LS 382 was the last original-spec National to submit to overhaul, being sent to Leyland at Nottingham in January 1986. One aesthetic change during 1985 had commercial implications; this was the creation of plastic frames into which were slotted card-backed segments of adverts, replacing the messy pasted bills that took paintwork off when

removed. Where LSs were concerned, their placement on bus sides blocked the roundel, which was invariably relocated towards the rear. Mobility Bus LSs 356 and 396 replaced LS 454 at Leyton in October, commencing new routes 921-926 on the 28th so that LS 454 could move to Ash Grove; capacity on all three was B21D+42 or five wheelchairs.

The massive programme of 2 November 1985 saw the 70 and 70A at Peckham and the 126 at Bromley converted from LS to T. One eye-opening change involving Nationals came about as the need to release some work from Barking after its takeup of most of the 5 upon its one-manning; the route involved was the 179, which was not only reallocated to Loughton and converted from T to LS operation but received an epic extension beyond Chingford to its new garage via roads not served by red buses in over a decade and a half. This was also the cue to pull back the 206's Epping leg for the winter, though (as usual) the garage journeys to Loughton were retained as part of its normal course to and from Grange Farm. Harrow Weald's situation was altered again with the conversion of the 209 to M upon its extension to Edgware; this obliged the official removal of all weekday M support from the 114, although enough were spare to double-deck the 136 on Saturdays to accompany its overall extension south to Northwick Park Hospital. This didn't last, the Saturday Ms being redeployed to the 258 from 14 December. LSs from Harrow Weald also occasionally appeared on the 140.

Above: **Aldenham's input into the LS story is illustrated on 30 May 1985 by LS 503 (GUW 503W), undergoing accident repair. It would not return to Walworth, instead going through the overhauling process once its repairs were finished, and after that it was outshopped to Ash Grove.** *John Laker*

Poplar was one of three garages to close. The 108 was transferred to Bow, introducing the class there in the form of LSs spare from Bromley's upgrade of the 126 to Titans, while three LS routes were put into West Ham, bringing the class back there in strength. One was the 276, which now took over the 56's roads to Beckton as an extension from Canning Town, though the gap from Poplar was not bridged. The D1, with its eye-catching LSs, also moved to West Ham, incorporating an extension from Seyssel Street to Poplar, Bazeley Street, and completing the trio was the S2. Instead of proceeding onward from Bromley-by-Bow Station to Poplar, it was

Right: **The D1 bounced about a bit in its short five years of existence. Its first transfer was on 2 November 1985 when Poplar closed and it took up at West Ham; although its custom-liveried LSs went with it, West Ham were apt to put out buses from their own fleet, such as LS 7 (KJD 507P) with white-on-black numberplate. In the background of this June 1986 shot, the Docklands Light Railway is going up, which would soon supersede the need for the D1.** *Haydn Davies*

now projected to Stratford and garage journeys
added onward from there to West Ham. The
Docklands Clipper-liveried LSs were now apt
to visit the 276 as well as existing West Ham
Titan routes 241 and 278, with Ts turning out
on the D1 in exchange, and the balance of
Poplar LSs furnished the 179 at Loughton. A
side-effect of the removal of Titans from Bow
(when the 10 passed from there to West Ham)
was the necessary conversion to LS of Bow's
ASDA free bus from Old Ford; this lasted till
December when Upton Park gained it with a T.
The N96, still the only LS-operated night route,
was revised in town to terminate at Waterloo
by taking the opposite direction from which it

had previously come. Meanwhile, the 256 at
Hornchurch was seeing more Ts than LSs, and
one 2 November change at Peckham was not
permanent but designed to fill in while the key
bridge linking Peckham to points north was
strengthened. Half the P3's service was rerouted
via St George's Way and given the number P2,
and this lasted for five months. Finally, the
eclectic tenure of National 2s at Stockwell came
to an end with the transfer of the 115 to Merton
and its concurrent takeover by standard LSs
(three coming in from overhaul). Bexleyheath
was now designated a storage site for surplus
LSs, taking a large number of Peckham buses
displaced from the 70 and 70A.

On 30 November the B1 at Bromley was converted from BL to LS operation, taking four of the buses stored at Bexleyheath; there were now very few BL-operated services left. Finally, Harrow Weald was still not satisfied with the spread of work afforded to its Ms and LSs; on 14 December the Saturday Ms were taken off the 136 and 209 and put back on the 114. And the poor 189 rounded out the year with the removal of its so recently-introduced short spurt to Tooting Broadway, terminating at the Mitre once again; outright withdrawal

had been on the cards, but outcry ensured the retention of this small portion at least.

1986 began with a major programme implemented on 1 February. The 12A's Sunday service now lost its projection between Croydon, Park Street and South Croydon, and the 202 at Hounslow was partially converted to LS due to the need to release Ms to Norbiton for the 65's one-manning; on 22 March this route was one of the first to be rerouted to serve the new Terminal 4 at Heathrow Airport. Its work done, the P2 came off on 4 May. The Thorpe Park

Left: **LS 9 (KJD 509P)** was one of the last eight LSs overhauled by Aldenham – this one actually done twice over its career – but on 14 November 1986 it is being inspected by dignitaries at Chiswick while serving as a trainer at Norbiton. In 1987 it would pass to Westlink and spend the next six years there. *John Laker*

Left: **LS 192 (THX 192S)** sees out Loughton garage's operations as it rounds Loughton station on 1 May 1986, three weeks before the end. After a year in storage, it would become one of the Mobility Bus conversions. *Haydn Davies*

extensions this year applied from 22 March, lasting until 28 September (216) and 19 October (216 and 218).

Repaints to LSs between overhaul commenced in February 1986 when LS 96 was treated at Aldenham, followed by LS 44 and a trickle thereafter. The four LSs made redundant from Stockwell were put into overhaul at this point (by Leyland at Nottingham), with plans to upseat five more from a growing number spare. But overhauls in the traditional sense were at an end, the last LS going through the process being LS 420, and from the National 2 contingent, LSs 470 and 472 (two of those upseated). Inevitably, the closure of Aldenham was announced in May, and even the contract overhauls had concluded by June; heavy maintenance was now the responsibility of the operating garages, and on a more regular basis. As 1986 progressed, Merton LSs were turning out on the 156 and making returns to the 57 (in exchange for DMS visits to the 152 and 189), with the odd Elmers End LS on that garage's Sunday allocation on the 75 and an Uxbridge LS or two filling in for a BL on the 128.

With the first six all sold, the second batch of LSs was now reaching its second decade and thus fell into consideration for sale; LSs 15 and 22 were sold in April and added to the British Airtours airside transfer fleet. Over fifty LSs were in store by April, most at AEC and Bexleyheath.

Tendering was now beginning to press at the edges of 'London Transport' and its red bus routes; the scheme based on Loughton wiped out almost all of its roster and the garage was closed on 24 May. 46 LSs were delicensed and kept on site until the garage was boarded up, following which they gathered at Aldenham. Passing to Eastern National Citybus, therefore, were routes 20, 167 and 206; the 201 took up with West's Coaches and the 250 and 250A (renumbered 251) departed the LRT network as wholly Essex County Council contracts operated by Sampson's. All of these used Nationals taken second-hand from one source or another.

The only Loughton route to survive as a red bus route was the most recent to have gone in; this was the 179 and this time it was reallocated to Leyton, retaining LSs, and only to fill the gap made by that garage's simultaneous loss of the 275 to Eastern National. New local route 179A was introduced, also with Leyton LSs, to cover the roads to the GLC border at Yardley Lane that were otherwise left fallow by the retraction of the 242 from the other direction. As the 179A was only Monday to Saturday, the 235 was extended up from Woodford Wells, performing a double-run to and from Chingford Station.

Another LS route was lost on 31 May; this was the 268, which departed Cricklewood for a new berth at London Country, which employed Iveco minibuses on it. On 21 June an extensive programme of one-manning was implemented, and loosely associated with it were alterations to the 12A, which was withdrawn on Sundays but replaced on that day by new route 12B, which took over the 59's Sunday-only projection beyond Purley to the border at Chipstead Valley. West Ham's 108 was rerouted at Blackheath to Lewisham rather than Eltham, making way for new route 286 over that section. The 210 was

reallocated from Muswell Hill to Holloway, taking on ex-Red Arrow or Stockwell National 2s (LSs 451, 459, 464, 470, 472, 473, 484-486, 488 and 489) upseated for the purpose, though three Mark Is came directly from Muswell Hill to help out; the balance of the Muswell Hill LSs went to Harrow Weald to allow an equivalent number of Ms to leave for Tottenham and thus increase LS appearances on the 209. Hornchurch's 244 was withdrawn and so was the 248A when it was decided to route the Corbets Tey service to Upminster Park Estate instead; as it passed under the low bridge, new route 246A needed LSs. The 246, meanwhile, found its evening service withdrawn between Harold Wood Station and Harold Hill. A rerouteing in Beckton took the 276 through revitalising areas filling with flats rather than the main Tollgate Road, and in a similarly growing area further to the west the D1 (passing with its dedicated fleet from West Ham to Bow, permitting visits to the 108 plus the return of the ASDA free bus ex-Upton Park) was taken out of its Poplar stand and its final leg rerouted to form a loop. Finally, not-quite-Red Arrow route 555 was withdrawn, no further subsidy from BR being forthcoming.

In July LSs 47 and 87 were licensed at Battersea for familiarisation, this garage having reopened not only as a base for the revamped Original London Sightseeing Tour but for a general storage site in replacement of Turnham Green. LS 258 was put into Croydon to train its drivers in preparation for the intake of the 12A and 12B after Elmers End's closure, even though LSs had only been away from Croydon for two years. During the summer 3,750 OPO London buses were fitted with assault screens.

On 2 August alterations to the 193 to accompany its conversion to minibus under Eastern National obliged the withdrawal of the 256, but it was on this day that one of the LSs' most spectacular tasks was set in motion. Seeing how tendering could grow operators as well as hack their routes away from them, LBL decided to take a punt on an ambitious route that covered a seemingly enormous swathe of inner Essex and commissioned new route X99, and marketed as 'The Forester.' Six LSs (27, 30, 71, 76, 79 and 435) recently out of overhaul but not allocated, were converted at Leyland's workshops in Nottingham to single-door specification with coach seating (DP42F) were put to work on a route that on Mondays to Fridays linked Harlow and Basildon via Epping, Loughton, Ilford, Romford, Brentwood and Billericay. Loadings on the first day were considerable, because it was advertised as free on its first day, but thereafter, despite the route being sensibly timed and operating on a half-hour frequency, it was subject to poor timekeeping and loadings fell off. LSs 118 and 121 substituted when needed.

London Buses had tried marketing its own special routes like the X99, but when it established Westlink it endeavoured to set up its own independent company. What it called Stanwell Buses Ltd was intended to be as remote from the style of London Transport as it could, with its own pay and terms but with the assurance of big backing from the parent if it needed it. On 9 August the 116, 117 and 203 were taken from their normal berth at Hounslow (which thus seamlessly absorbed two routes from the closed Southall garage), and their given a white-and-green stripe down their midriffs upon their move into a new industrial-estate premises at Pulborough Way, Hounslow Heath (unofficially coded WK but never displayed as such on any buses operated); this was the location of the base and head office, with the actual open-field storage at Falcon Way. 28 LSs (13, 24, 29, 40, 67, 99, 116, 145, 150, 153, 157, 161, 195, 206, 251, 257, 270, 297, 304, 317, 335, 337, 373, 385, 408, 429, 431 and 434) made the move on lease from LBL to Stanwell Buses Ltd and most would complete long spells there, especially when Westlink started bidding for Surrey tenders later in the decade.

In contrast to the X99, Westlink was as simple an aesthetic as you could get, consisting of simply ripping the roundels off two dozen Hounslow LSs and unrolling a two-tone vinyl strip along their midsection instead, to create the illusion to passengers that this was no longer staid old London Transport but a new and exciting independent. The punters may or may not have swallowed it, but Westlink ended up outliving all four of its similarly-inspired successors (Kingston Buses, Harrow Buses, Bexleybus and Suttonbus). Now based at an open-field site west of Hounslow Heath but never to carry its 'WK' code are LS 145 (THX 145S) in Bedfont and LS 431 (BYW 431V) in Ashford, both photographed in October 1986. Both: *Haydn Davies*

Right: **Minibuses may have been flavour of the month within London Buses Ltd by 1986, but their capacity was inferior on some sections of route otherwise treated. Accordingly, when new route R5 replaced former London Country SNB route 431 upon the introduction of the Roundabout minibus network on 16 August 1986, a peak-hour journey with a Bromley LS was included. Seen with two numbers on display in the first month of operation is LS 406 (BYW 406V).** *Haydn Davies*

Right: **The H1 out of Harrow Weald was extended to Northwick Park Hospital on 16 August 1986, and that October is seen in the hands of LS 388 (BYW 388V), halfway through a two-year spell at the garage.** *Haydn Davies*

Right: **The commercial imperative unleashed on D-Day prompted LBL to send out probes to the south into Surrey. The 306 was a straight copy of London & Country's 406 between Kingston and Epsom, but it wasn't a success, even though at least a couple of people have taken advantage of Norbiton's LS 381 (BYW 381V) that November.** *Haydn Davies*

Orpington's tendered network bowed a week later, on the 16th, but the only knock-on effect to LSs was the loss of the 61 to Metrobus and the withdrawal of the 284. One of the new minibus services, however, did warrant the addition of peak-hour LS journeys provided by Bromley; this was the R5 replacing most of London Country's 471 as a circular between Orpington and Cudham. Harrow Weald's H1 on the other side of town was projected from Northwick Park Station to the hospital, and on 23 August the 236 was rerouted to squeeze its way through Pownall Road, a narrow but very heavily populated residential section of Hackney.

The final OPO programme of 1986 was executed on 25 October and hit twelve routes, with the appropriate ripples affecting our LSs. As part of the 12's retraction towards town, the 12A was increased in scope with an extension from Forest Hill to Peckham that was also included in the 12B's remit. Both routes, plus the 289, were reallocated to Croydon upon the closure of Elmers End. Indeed the 194 was earmarked for full conversion to LS upon its own reallocation to Croydon, but even though this used up some of the stored stock at Aldenham, mixed DMS and LS operation prevailed. At Norbiton, the 216 was withdrawn on Sundays, and its partner 218 was taken out of the network altogether upon its transfer to London Country South West. Catford's LSs commenced new shoppers' service L1 on Saturdays linking unserved sections of Brockley and Grove Park via Deptford and Lewisham. On 15 November an L2 was added on Saturdays for Christmas, also LS from Catford but a circular service taking passengers from the outer sections of the Downham estate to Lewisham and back. In order to make use of some more of the now embarrassingly large surfeit of LSs and release Ts to Chalk Farm for the 24 and new 168, the 56 at West Ham was demoted from T to LS operation, any Titans it saw thereafter coming as cross-links from the 10 and 225.

The deregulation of all bus services outside London was implemented on 26 October 1986, and even with troubles of its own as it was compelled to decline, LBL had another try at an all-encompassing commercial service on 27 October with new routes 306 and 310A, this time entering into direct competition with services operated by London Country successors. The first linked Kingston and Epsom with Norbiton LSs and the latter Enfield Town and Hertford with LSs drafted into Potters Bar as early as 1 October. The 310A's Nationals soon drifted to the 84, long since taken out of the LRT network but treated very much like a normal red route since its return to Potters Bar on 21 June, plus the 242 and 263, and by the end of the year, the W8.

Above: **On 21 June 1986 the Sunday projection of the 59 to Chipstead Valley was pulled back to Purley due to congestion further north preventing its serving efficiently. Instead the area was linked to the 12A, already going only as far as Purley on Sundays as it was. The resulting 12B was later transferred from Elmers End to Croydon when the former garage closed on 25 October 1986, and the following month in the Brighton Road, we see LS 110 (THX 110S). A handwritten placard to reflect the simultaneous extension of both 12A and 12B to Peckham is carried until blinds with the new destination are printed.**
Haydn Davies

Right: **The 56 proved a little ahead of its time, as the Beckton regions it served were still abandoned dockyards and not yet upmarket flats. Accordingly it was demoted to LS operation to release Titans needed more urgently elsewhere, and withdrawn outright soon after that. On 12 February 1987 West Ham's LS 33 (KJD 533P), freshly come from Norbiton and still carrying its garage codes, awaits the off at Aldgate.** *John Laker*

In preparation for the closure of Aldenham on 15 November, half the stock of stored LSs were divided between available space at Edgware, Fulwell and West Ham, but plans were simultaneously being drawn up to re-use the 33 remaining spare ones on less favoured routes so that their double-deckers could be released to convert ever more, and increasingly central, Routemaster-operated routes to OPO. LS 393 was the last Leyland National repaint done at Aldenham. Security problems arising from this dispersal, not to mention the willingness of sectors of society to resort to vandalism, resulted in an arson attack on West Ham on 6 November which destroyed LSs 32 and 364 and damaged LSs 151 and 200. Already stripped

LS 185 was deleted finally from stock, while LS 16 was sold. When Aldenham finally closed its doors, its stored LSs were sent to AEC, with a handful each squeezing in at Cricklewood and Turnham Green. A spray booth was set up at Chiswick for when general repaints could be resumed in-house, but presentation fleetwide started to decline alarmingly despite the savings made from closing Aldenham and laying off its workforce. Reflecting societal trends along the same manner, the fleet as a whole had perspex anti-assault screens fitted to driver's cabs during the second half of 1986. At the end of the year Eastbourne Buses was contracted to carry out maintenance to LSs and sixteen, mostly from AEC stock of long-term sick buses, travelled to their premises, before the new spray booth at Chiswick got going in earnest during 1987.

The loop idea for the end of the D1 hadn't taken, and it was rerouted from 22 November to terminate at Queen Hotel. On 29 November Uxbridge sent two BLs to Holloway to form extras on the C11, taking in exchange Mark 2 LS 464 to provide variety on the 98, 204 and 224; this attempt to upgrade the Hillingdon Local 128 from BL to LS didn't catch on, however, and BLs were back in ten days. Routine strange workings for the latter portion of 1986 included multiple Norbiton LSs on the 71, 85 and even the 213, plus Uxbridge LSs drifting to M-operated 222. Despite there being 80 LSs in store, shortages began to bite, with Croydon barely able to muster the 289's runout in advance of its impending loss on tender and Victoria having to take upseated LS 486 on loan from Holloway and fit it with a farebox to put out on the Red Arrows.

Below: **The 71's Sunday service had been OMO for some time before the conversion of the rest of the route, and between 4 September 1982 and 14 January 1984 had been officially LS-operated. After the one-manning with Ms, LSs were still apt to appear, and LS 410 (BYW 410V) is doing just that at Kingston in June 1986.** *Haydn Davies*

Left: **The 194 had seen a good deal of LS operation during the middle portion of the 1980s and so followed its Sunday-only offshoot 194A, introduced on 27 April 1985 so that Shirley Way could retain buses on that day of the week after the withdrawal of the 119B. Croydon's LS 103 (OJD 903R), also seen on the cover when a Bromley bus and well-known on the preservation circuit today, is seen in August 1987.** *Haydn Davies*

On 7 December the 194A was converted to LS operation, necessitating the printing of blinds with the suffix on the main panel. The following day saw the Saturday shoppers' services L1 and L2 added on Mondays to Fridays with financial backing from the London Borough of Lewisham until Christmas, when the L2 came off and the L1 reverted to Saturdays only. Revisions to the Mobility Bus services on 8 December took off the 902, 903, 904, 925 and 926 and introduced new routes 928, 947, 948, 966 and 973. LS 105 was converted to wheelchair accessibility at PMT during November to become the fourth LS so equipped, and it went to Ash Grove.

Below: **London Regional Transport Promotion Bus 1234L (SCO 422L) is seen on 19 February 1987 in the company of single-deck RM 1368.** *John Laker*

As 1987 opened, the need to implement ever more OPO conversions remained as strong as ever, though for the first time there was no yearly order of new double-deckers with which to do it, so the strategy was now to furnish them through tendering losses and through the re-use of the large surplus of LSs piling up around the system. On 3 February the 160 at Catford was accordingly demoted from T to LS (using ten of those treated at Eastbourne and allowing Ts to depart for the 30 at Clapton), and the large 7 February programme forced the 124 to take on LSs on Sundays as well. Although enough new Ls were now arriving at Croydon to render single-deck operation

on the 194 and 194A more random than it had been hoped, the 166 was now officially single-decked, using the LSs made spare by the 289's loss on this day to London Country South West but taking a fortnight or so to bed in as the main component. West Ham's 241 and 278 were also partially converted to LSs to release enough Ts for the one-manning of the 30 at Clapton, and the one-bus 299 fell thus in its entirety. As one of the facets of LRT planning at this point in time was to convert crew routes to OPO on Sundays, many thus fell on this day and the 55 was one of them, but the continued lack of double-deckers at Leyton meant that LSs had to step in. Reductions to the 202 at Hounslow

saw its Twickenham-Richmond service cut at evenings and outside peak hours, and finally both the 306 and X99, after such bright hopes as LBL's ambassadors beyond its borders into the wild maelstrom of the post-deregulation arena, were withdrawn without replacement.

The second and third week of January 1987 saw some wintry weather descend on London and the south-east, being perhaps the last prolonged such instance in this generation. Ash Grove suffered difficulties with the Titans based on the 106 and instead deputised National 2s on this route on six separate days, just one of them displaying other than the three-track route number. At the other end of the Red Arrow network, Victoria couldn't start any LSs at all on 14 January and, in order to keep the 507 functioning, had to borrow an OV minibus from the basement! The snow was just as bad that day in south London, enough to oblige Peckham to stick an LS out on the 63.

On 16 February the LS workings on the 241 and 278 were switched to the 10, demoting that route from Titan despite its important

role in central London. Already hacked down in scope and converted to LS, the 56 was now withdrawn on 28 February outside Monday-to-Friday peak hours and the 278 extended west to Aldgate in its stead; the 276 lost its evening service. Desperate for Titans as 1987 progressed, LBL had to pick routes that it didn't think would feel their loss too badly, and, just as in 1979 after DMSs, the 126 was chosen for reversion to LS with effect from 7 March. On the other side of town, the 207 needed so many Metrobuses that adjacent local routes had to be similarly stripped; on 14 March the 112 and 245 at Cricklewood were converted to LS and on the 28th, the day the 207 finally went OPO after two postponements, the 98 and 224 at Uxbridge lost their element of double-deck support to supply the needed Ms. Hounslow was given a daily LS roster in support of Uxbridge, covering a new allocation on the 98 on weekdays and the 223 on Sundays (replacing the withdrawal of the 202 on this day of the week). A week later, this latter working officially assumed Ms and the 98 continued to see them from both garages. A similar relaxation allowed the 124 and 160 to regain Sunday Ts from 26 April. There could have been even more demotions, the 240 and 288 at Edgware having long been pencilled in for LSs but in event remaining M-operated.

At Hounslow, its LSs made forays to the 237 now that it had been converted to OPO, and

then to the 232 and 120. The 190 at Croydon saw its first LS on 13 February, as did the 130 just once. The X99's LSs were dispersed, LS 76 heading to Leyton for private-hire work (plus one documented visit to the 230 on 14 March) and LSs 27, 30 and 435 passing to Battersea for preparation for similar use, being repainted to red in April; the other two remained at Hornchurch for spare use on the 246 before leaving in March (LS 71 to Leyton and LS 79 to Battersea, at which point LS 76 was transferred from Leyton to Battersea). It was at this point that the wheelchair-equipped LSs at Ash Grove and Leyton (the latter's turning out on the 179A during their downtime) were formally christened with Mobility Bus fleetnames. Leyland National production having given way to the Lynx in 1985, an example of the newest Leyland single-decker was borrowed and turned out on the 70 and P3 at Peckham between 9 and 27 February. Four LSs were sold to Eastbourne during the month and two more in April, these serving as part-payment for the heavy refurbishments to the LSs that had gone back into service at Catford and Bromley, and LS 398 at Hounslow was fitted out as an inspector's hut at the bus station following the demolition by a bus of the existing structure!

March saw LSs 170 and 399 delicensed at Holloway, theoretically bringing to an end appearances of Mk I LSs on the 210, but things were never that simple and by the end of the decade, all notions of standardisation would fall by the wayside. On 14 April the five LSs

Below: **The X99 had proven a spectacular failure, leaving six converted LSs with nothing to do but turn out on Leyton's regular 179A until more appropriate work could be found for them. In April 1987 LS 71 (OJD 871R) drifts down Station Road in Chingford.** *Haydn Davies*

now gathered at Battersea and now all in red joined a host of other eclectic vehicles to take up a contract in the name of London Coaches for the Japanese School Ltd, transporting pupils from central London to the Acton area.

For the first time, no buses were on order for 1987, LRT and LBL gambling on being able to furnish requirements in the short term with the buses displaced from tendering. They also were forced to the unimaginable step of buying second-hand, as were the independents, and in the case of the nine Van Hool-McArdle-bodied ex-South Yorkshire PTE Volvo Ailsas added to the V class at Potters Bar in March (via Ensign), they were part-exchanged for twelve LSs mostly selected from stored examples at Edgware but in the event not to actually leave stock for another year. One of the interesting features of the new (old) Vs was their elegant 'Leaside' livery that added a broad white band and black skirt to the existing red. Potters Bar, being closer exposed to radical provincial ideas than any other 'LT' garage, was tempted to spread it, LS 112 being the first in May. When the 107 came in from Edgware on 6 June, LSs soon made their appearance.

In May LS 13 at Westlink was treated to a revised livery in which the white-turquoise-white central band was upswept over the rear in white; it was also named Chamberlain Diplomat. 17 May saw the 116's Thorpe Park summer Sunday extension return, rather later than usual (this year applying until 27 September), while on 23 May Potters Bar's LSs commenced a Sunday commercial service numbered 318 based on Waltham Cross; it was successful enough for a weekday service to be added on 27 July. You could tell whether the bus had been on the 310A as the '3' and '1' were squeezed on the first track so as to permit the suffix letter on the third. It was better than the previous expedient of printing a tiny 'A' bang in the middle of the '0'!

Finally, and not a moment too soon, double-deck OPO buses returned to Leyton garage when the 55 was one-manned on 6 June. As well as this route, the 97A, 230 and N96 were converted from LS to T, which more than made up for the pulling back of the 97A from Hackney to Leyton Green. Changes to Peckham's 70 and 70A, using some of the former Leyton LSs, reconfigured the latter into a daily LS-operated circular penetrating Nunhead and Brockley and taking over the parent during evenings and weekends (but only as far as Waterloo). This allowed the P3 to disengage from its circular role and push out of the area to terminate at New Cross garage (additionally converting from LS to T operation at weekends). Underscoring the provision of services to the Surrey Docks area

Above: **LS 324 (AYR 324T) operated out of Potters Bar between October 1986 and September 1987. Its route 310A was the lone success story of the commercial services mounted upon Deregulation Day and lasted a decade and a half.**
Haydn Davies

(shortly to become known as Surrey Quays to cement its emergence from a long period of decline), the 181 was projected over the 70 round the peninsula to Rotherhithe; at its other end it was rerouted to approach Catford from the other direction. In the same area the 108B was converted to LS on Sundays, and at the north-eastern extremity of London, Leyton's 179A received a Sunday service to offset the 235's withdrawal on that day of the week. The 236 was extended ambitiously past Leytonstone to Walthamstow Central to support the 235 and replace the 97A over its withdrawn section, and finally for 27 June a Mobility Bus network for south-and south-east London was introduced, based around three new conversions in the form of Peckham's LS 139, 293 and 320 (with help at first from LS 396 on loan) and featuring new routes 931-933, 936, 937 and 970. These conversions introduced green handrails now familiar on the Ls and DMS 2456. MCW was charged with the conversion of three more (LSs 256, 290 and 308) and another trio was at AEC ready to follow them; all of these plus the existing ones were formally transferred during July into the ownership of LRT's Disabled Unit.

One new route accruing to LS visits was the 183, put into Harrow Weald on 6 June upon Hendon's closure and otherwise M-operated. The 299 at West Ham was another one to chalk up, seen on 13 June, while multiple rail jobs over the summer saw the use of several east London garages' LSs, including the Docklands Clipper ones. LS 71 at Leyton held on to its Forester

livery, but otherwise, repainting was stepping up, a new and increasingly prolific contractor to this task being Gatwick Engineering. In the summer a new London Buses roundel with a yellow bar over a white circle was introduced and began spreading across the fleet. Though it barely mattered any more with tendering scything through LBL's established patterns and more devolution looming, Abbey District was deleted on 15 August.

What was later to be known as Kingston Bus was to prove one of the most difficult experiences LRT would suffer with tendering. Amid the strikes that bedevilled the controversial reintroduction of standard DMSs to the fleet when the network made its bow on 27 June, Norbiton's LSs had their say, being kept despite the loss of the 215 to join the new mixed fleet of DMSs and remaining Ms on the 71, 85 and 213 while DMSs took their time being prepared for service. In the debits column for Norbiton fell the 131 (lost to London Country South West) and 215. This route was renumbered K3 as a Westlink service and was given an LS component from the outset, on a temporary basis until the intended MCW Metrorider minibuses (MRs) were ready, two weeks or so later. Kingston was the operating garage, reopened once again after three years. The 216 (operated from this point as a commercial service) lost its leg to Tolworth Broadway but the 152 gained an extension west to Kingston rather than getting on the A3 to Surbiton (or Chessington Zoo) as before.

On 11 July, as part of a raft of changes that saw the 43 and 49 one-manned, the 156's projections south to Morden were localised as new route 163 from Merton. There was no reason why it should have been LS from the outset, but more were available than there were DMSs, and four of the five needed were made available by partially double-decking the 166 at Croydon and transferring the 189 from Merton to Stockwell, which allotted it a single DMS. Merton's resulting surplus of LSs were apt to turn out on the 57.

The closure of Clapton garage on 15 August obliged many of its routes to pass to Ash Grove, so to clear the space Walworth was reactivated as a Red Arrow-only garage, this time coded RA. In with their National 2s went the 500 and 507 from Victoria as well as the 501, 502 and 513 from Ash Grove. At the same time a sixth Red Arrow route was added; numbered 509, it was a between-peaks and Saturdays link from Liverpool Street to Oxford Street, returning in a loop via Piccadilly. 55 LSs in total were now based, LSs 468 and 487 coming in a little later due to mechanical attention at Stockwell (a fellow Wandle garage, unlike Camberwell, which despite being literally over the road, was part of Selkent!). Until pooled blinds could be printed, the ex-Ash Grove buses working on ex-Victoria routes and vice versa had to go around with just numbers.

Even before the fallout from the Norbiton operation had settled, LBL was planning two more area-based tendering networks, and this time both would have new liveries. Bexleybus, the second of the two and planned for January 1988 implementation, had a superb blue and cream livery chosen; not coincidentally, that

was the livery at the time of Eastbourne Buses, which was contracted to paint these and other LSs not going to Gatwick Engineering. LS 82 was the first in during August, to form a single-deck complement of about two dozen on four of the network's routes.

The 216 was transferred on 19 September from Norbiton to Kingston as a Westlink route; following on the heels of LSs 9 and 41 (transferred to Stanwell Buses on 22 June), LSs 268, 314, 381 and 422 were transferred on 24 September, the intention being to release an equivalent number for permanent basing at Kingston, although in practice LSs were pooled with the main body at Hounslow Heath, and interestingly, the six transferred examples had their assault screens removed when they went. Due to brake drum problems with the Metroriders belonging to the K2 and K3, LSs were apt to appear on those routes. On 17 October Leyton lost the 179 and 179A, both of which passed to Grey-Green on tender and released its LSs for Bexleybus preparation at Eastbourne, together with some ex-Norbiton examples as DMSs got established there. The 236 managed to get even further, taking over the 212 on Sundays as far as Chingford Station. On 31 October Leyton found itself dabbling in Essex County Council contracts through the taking up of the 500's Sunday service between Romford and Harlow.

Strange workings for the autumn of 1987 put Leyton's remaining LSs, somewhat ludicrously, onto the 38, not just on its Sunday OPO roster introduced on 6 June, but at least once on the weekday service with a conductor! LS 126 of this garage was part of a three-bus pool at Forest District whereby, together with LS 46 (West Ham) and LS 151 (Hornchurch), they would be used at the district's garages as needed. The relicensing of LS 199 at Holloway in September brought Mark I LSs back to the 210, while at the same time that route's Mark 2s began straying to the 271.

If Kingston Bus was bad, Harrow Buses were worse, at least in popular estimation. The scheme, set going on 14 November 1987, exchanged Harrow Weald's Ms for second-hand Volvos and leased Mark II Metrobuses (as they appeared), but retained an LS component. While officially coming off the 114, 136 and 209, the LSs stayed on the H1 after its reconfiguration as circular services 201 and 211, settled on the 258 and started off the 340 while the new Ms were awaited. In truth, everything appeared on everything sooner or later; better any bus than no bus! The livery, however, proved to be a winner, adding a broad cream band amidships; LSs 278 and 325 were the first to go into it, but were the only two carrying it on the network's debut and remained so by year's end. Released by hired ex-GM Buses Daimler

Above: **The smart and straightforward Harrow Buses livery belied a raft of problems at the new network. LS 278 (YYE 278T), seen in November 1987 shortly before the H1 was recast as circular pair 201 and 211, was one of only two LSs to be carrying the new livery by the end of 1987, and the fleetname transfers haven't made their appearance yet. This bus had come to Harrow Weald after overhaul in October 1984 and would serve here for the rest of its career.**
Haydn Davies

Right: **Leaside livery was all the rage during 1987 as this LBL district sought to at least loosen the aesthetic chains that a decade of all-red livery had imposed. It wasn't as imposing adding a black skirt and broad white band on LSs as it was on the district's Ms, but it caught eyes nonetheless. Potters Bar's LS 112 (THX 112S) was the inaugural repaint, and is seen on the 310A (disregard the blinds) in September 1988.**
Haydn Davies

Right: **Subtly tweaking traditional red in the manner of Leaside Buses and Harrow Buses was one thing, but with Bexleybus LBL wanted to dispel from passengers' minds that this was actually a 'red bus' operation all along. The blue and cream livery, applied under contract by Eastbourne Buses, which enjoyed the same combination of colours, was the best part of Bexleybus, whose struggles were legend. The unit even had its own parallel fleetnumbers, which meant that LS 73 (OJD 873R) was also known as plain 46. It is seen in April 1988 on new route 422, the former eastern end of the old 122 and emphatically too busy for single-deckers.**
Haydn Davies

Right: **LS 155 (THX 155S), also pictured in April 1988, was known as 52 while at Bexleyheath, and one of its jobs was on the 492, a former Kentish Bus route operating mostly within the London border and therefore game to be taken into the network.**
Haydn Davies

Fleetlines, three of the spare Harrow Weald LSs were sent to Holloway to commence replacing (on the 21st) the Mark 2s on the 210, which were going to be needed for new Red Arrow route 510 commencing on 16 January 1988. In December, nine more LSs left Harrow Weald, five going into Holloway to continue the 210 (and now making the 271's oddments Mark Is) and four to Potters Bar. Their work done as the full complement of DMSs settled in at Norbiton on the 71, 85 and 213, the garage's remaining LS were scheduled to depart on 21 November; LSs 184 and 186 were the last ones out, on the 30th. The 65 had remained steadfastly M but on 13 October LS 328 appeared while it still could.

21 November's programme finished off the 56 and pulled the 278 back to Limehouse from the east. Hounslow's 257 was withdrawn through its absorption into an extension of the 120.

Despite the fanfare given to the liveries for Harrow Buses and Bexleybus, LBL as a whole was thinking about an improved image after the praise given to its Leaside livery (of which LS 112 was the sole recipient so far), and in December Peckham's LS 403 became the first National to go into 'tapegrey', LBL's new livery. On the LS, the white band of the livery was carried above the windows. Publicity of a different kind came through the application of adverts to the roof panels of Leyton's LS fleet in November so that office workers in tower blocks could look down from their windows and consider buying the products of IBM, this particular sponsor. LSs 227 and 411 at West Ham were also treated, but the former was repainted by the end of the year and lost its particular ad.

1988 kicked off with the extension on 2 January of the 224 from Stockley Estate to the new Stockley Park Business Park. It was on the 16th that Bexleybus, the most notorious of all the area-based tendering networks made its debut, and as with the others, LSs had their part to play. In this case twenty-four of them were part of the new operation under the plain numbers 41-64, comprising in age order LSs 18, 21, 28, 31, 50, 73, 82, 120, 126, 135, 137, 155, 178, 184, 186, 239, 282, 284, 294, 315, 316, 328, 329 and 428. Their final preparations were carried out at Gatwick Engineering through the fitting of radios and Wayfarer ticket machines, including Autocheck equipment which reduced their capacity from B36D to B34D, and when they arrived they were allocated as the main complement for routes 422 and 492, the former taking over the 122's eastern extremity and the latter copying much of its Kentish Bus predecessor to take LRT services to Dartford from a second direction. Bexleybus's LSs also took over the 269 from the closed Sidcup's Titans and Olympians and operated the 244 and 291 pair in and out of Woolwich, though inevitably all would turn out where needed on any of the 96, 99, 178, 229, 272, 401 and 469. LS 329 (or 63) had to wait, as its engine seized on the way from Eastbourne to Bexleyheath.

Above: **After Leaside, Harrow Buses and Bexleybus came plain old tapegrey, the livery settled on by LBL to take it into the 1990s, when deregulation was still anticipated (or dreaded, depending on which side of London bus operations' financial equation you found yourself). Surprisingly dull by comparison with some of the schemes appearing across the country as deregulation threw into contention the entire ethos of bus operation, tapegrey nonetheless suited the generally straight lines of the Leyland National, and LS 379 (BYW 379V) out of Hounslow is no exception. The effect was topped off by a new roundel, whose bar was yellow with 'LONDON BUSES' in red thereon. There were the odd exceptions, of course; Croydon's Ls 128 had the grey skirt up to and over the wheelarches, but the concept marked a return to some sense of standardisation where anything but had been the case since tendering began.**
Haydn Davies

The 10 was withdrawn after a long decline, but its unique central links across the Elephant were not replaced; instead from the west, new Red Arrow route 510 was commissioned to link Victoria and Aldgate (adding to the overall complement the ex-Holloway National 2s, which retained their upseated configuration and indeed worked this way on all of Walworth's Red Arrow routes), and at the extreme other end the 108 was projected from Stratford to Wanstead. Neither was quite adequate and would both come off long before their time. The 108 and D1 were also reallocated from Bow to West Ham to cover the loss of the 10 and free space at Bow for the massive increase that accompanied the one-manning of the 25. That was the end of LSs at Bow, and also, unfortunately, of the Docklands Clipper livery. LSs 53 and 260 were repainted immediately upon transfer to West Ham (the former receiving tapegrey), and the other three went into store at the back of Fulwell, one of the most recent storage sites identified. West Ham's new intake quickly started making appearances on the 262 and 8A and was firmly established by now as the majority allocation on the 278, with more than a few on the 241. Lastly, Catford's Saturday L1 was withdrawn from Grove Park but rerouted via Hilly Fields.

Beginning in February, Harrow Weald's LSs started a repaint programme to get them all into the livery of that operation, as part of an increase to repaints in general that also spread the new tapegrey across the fleet even as plans were drawn up to further subdivide LBL into eleven self-standing units in advance of deregulation (which by mid-1988 had drifted to beyond the mooted date of 1990). In many cases the skirt and band were applied over existing red or recent red repaints; Westlink's triple stripe was a vinyl rather than painted. One new subcontractor for heavier maintenance was Southend Transport, which repaired LS 445's engine in January 1988. Not only did LSs return to Norbiton in February in the form of LSs 130 and 181, but the latter was still in Docklands Clipper livery, albeit with its logo replaced by the new 'Kingston Bus' vinyl in yellow and red. Bromley sent out LS 69 to help Orpington on the R1 on 12 February, while the Lewisham Centrelink route saw Peckham's Mobility Bus LSs out alongside BLs 36 and 81. With LS blinds at Uxbridge now including the 207, LS 229 as UX135 on 28 March became the first on that extremely busy route. LS firsts this spring were on the C11 (LS 39 on 18 May) and 262A (19 June, though able only to display '262'); appearances continued on Potters Bar's 107, Leyton's 230 and Hounslow's 232.

Try as they might, LT and its successors have never quite been able to make unidirectional circular services work, and as quickly as 23 January the 201/211 pair were consolidated to work in both directions under the number 201. Isolated cuts from 26 March took off the Eltham-Woolwich leg of the 126 during evenings and the Saturday service on the 509, while there was still a demand for a schoolday service to Hook that the 152 had historically performed, so one was reinstated on 11 April. On 26 March the Mobility Bus services operated by Ash Grove (routes 921-924 and 928) were transferred with their LSs (105 and 454) to Leyton; on the same day LSs 256 and 308 were added to Peckham, while other LSs remained stored at

MCW to be converted if demand arose. The London Coaches fleet, including the five LSs on the Japanese School contract, moved from Battersea to Wandsworth between 6 and 16 April, and over the Easter weekend Fulwell came into use as LBL's permanent sales stock base in replacement of AEC's old site; ironically, to clear the site for the 100 RMs coming in, five of the 14 LSs already there had to move to AEC! They were joined at AEC by three (LSs 156, 192 and 202) earmarked for future Mobility Bus use. When the old AEC site was vacated as demanded by the end of May, the remaining stored LSs were sold to Ensign, which, having won a raft of tenders that would put an end to Hornchurch garage in the autumn, had plans of its own for them. 4 June saw the 276 and 278 swap their eastern ends so that the former now got through to North Woolwich rather than East Beckton, now the terminus of the unofficial but dominant horde of LSs on the latter!

On 30 May Potters Bar commenced another season on the 318, now dubbed Lea Valley Leisure Bus and set going with LS 175 specially repainted with black skirt and white midriff (enclosing a thin red band). National 2 operation at Holloway finally came to an end on 17 May, and big things were in store for the three holdouts (LSs 451, 488 and 489) plus one transferred up from Walworth (LS 483). With the intent to use them (plus similarly-customised four-speed Metrobuses) on a contract to and from Alexandra Palace, Leaside District fitted coach seating; the work was done at Holloway (LSs 483 and 488) and at Wood Green (LSs 451 and 489). When not needed on their respective gigs, Wood Green turned its new acquisitions out on the 221, 144A and 141 and Holloway allowed its pair to make return appearances to the 210 and 271. LS 489 was even loaned to Merton in June! Westlink was also progressing; in April LS 24 was treated to the livery already

Left: **March 1988 saw Harrow Weald's LS 310 (AYR 310T) repainted into Harrow Buses livery following an uptick in the programme, and all were done by July. The network featured blinds in all upper-case, a throwback which was more attractive and informative but not to last.** *Haydn Davies*

Left: **The enhanced Leaside livery applied to LS 175 (THX 175S) in 1988 was not dissimilar to that of Harrow Buses, other than adding another red band in the body seam. Intended for the 310A out of Potters Bar, it was inevitable that it would wander, and is see doing just that on the W8 at Winchmore Hill.** *Jim Blake*

on LS 13. Five more were repainted in May and another two in June. Even the Red Arrow brand was being freshened along these lines, LS 495 being the first (in June) to take on a tapegrey variant where the forward edge was shaped like an arrow. And finally, the repaint of Harrow Weald's LSs into Harrow Buses livery (a task carried out at Edgware) was drawing to a close; the full complement numbered LSs 34, 48, 234, 246, 248, 249, 263, 278, 285, 310, 321, 325, 331, 352, 387, 402, 407 and 416. LSs 102 and 119 served as the repaint float, leaving in August after the last repaint (to LS 285) was completed in July.

Despite having been burned with the 306, Norbiton decided to have another crack at the Surrey commercial market and introduced new route K10 on 11 July under the Kingfisher brand. Several more incoming LSs from a variety of sources (but mostly Cricklewood) solidified the return of the type, including Docklands Clipper-liveried LS 165 to join LS 171 already based; three more had a black skirt added and on all of them the 'K' of the route number was in red on the white of the first number track. Linking Kingston and Staines, the eight-bus K10 was determined to serve almost every locality in between! There then came rather more

Left: **On 8 June 1988 two of the 128's three intended LSs are being finished at Chiswick, ready to replace the BLs still at work on that route.** *John Laker*

ceremony than was usual for a vehicle upgrade when at midday on 13 July BLs 56 and 93-95 were formally replaced on the Hillingdon Local 128 and 128A by LSs 222, 236 and 240, repainted into a similarly yellow-accented livery (but adding the now familiar grey skirt) at Chiswick during June; a photo-call was arranged at Uxbridge Civic Centre before they went out. The three Nationals had been purchased by the London Borough of Hillingdon at a cost of £11,000 each to be leased back to LBL to operate

on their behalf until two new Leyland Lynxes on order were delivered. As it happened, the three Nationals would last only two years and the route itself not much longer than that, but for the moment, once blinds were fitted (white-on-black rather than the yellow-on-green of the outgoing BLs), the LSs popped up on the 204, 222 and 223. As had their BL predecessors, they wore adverts for E&O Motors of Ruislip behind the wheelarches. Existing Uxbridge LSs continued to visit the 207 (as they had to the 128

Left: **And in service during August, following the handover ceremony on 13 July. This is LS 222 (THX 222S), previously of Croydon. Blinds with Johnston font are now fitted, an affectation which would spread over the next few years as the factory-fitted blinds wore out with use.** *Haydn Davies*

Right: **Tapegrey livery application sometimes omitted the tape, as on Cricklewood's LS 372 (BYW 372V) at Ealing Broadway in July 1988. The 112 had been converted to LS to release Metrobuses for the one-manning of the 207 the previous spring.**
Haydn Davies

Right: **On 1 August 1989 nine more Mobility Bus routes were introduced, based on a swathe of north-west London within reach of the operating garage at Cricklewood. LS 308 (AYR 308T) is setting off from Northwick Park Hospital in October.**
Haydn Davies

Right: **The 500 had been the perfect Red Arrow route, speeding passengers from the rail hub at Victoria to their workplaces in Oxford Street without any fuss (and without any seats either, if you didn't bag the 24 at the back fast enough), but following its withdrawal on 13 August 1988, successive attempts to pick up its slack fell victim to one unsuccessful tinkering after the next. Just such was the 509, which was reconfigured from a loop to a normal service and ultimately withdrawn. In July 1988 LS 462 (GUW 462W) is coming round Marble Arch.**
Haydn Davies

and 128A in latter BL days), and across town Bexleyheath's 96 was a common spot for them as well as fellow intended double-deck route 272. On 16 July the R5's Bromley LS-operated journeys were separated out under their own new identity as 471. On 30 July the 112 was lost to Atlas Bus, four of its LS fleet at Cricklewood already having been transferred away to furnish the K10 at Norbiton and thus replaced until the end by Ms.

Mobility Bus services continued to expand and change; LSs 156, 192, 202 and 308 were converted to wheelchair accessibility and sent to Cricklewood on 1 August for the unveiling of nine new routes numbered 981-989, operated with the financial assistance of the London Borough of Brent. LS 308 had previously worked at Peckham in the same role.

After 22 years, the original Red Arrow route, 500, was withdrawn on 13 August 1988. Created to help start the reduction of crew operation, it was ironic that it was replaced directly by the strongest remaining crew route of all, the 73, as a diversion to Victoria. The 509 was amended to terminate at Oxford Circus rather than carry out a loop, and two new services were introduced; the 503 linking South Kensington and Russell Square and 506 between Victoria and Paddington. The 510 received a short extension from Aldgate to the DLR terminus at Tower Gateway. This date was when the garage finally applied 'RA' codes to its buses, a year since reopening; repaints were done at

Merton and then Walworth staff added the tape band and grey skirt. At Peckham, the 70 in its final months found itself partially converted to LS, taking six of them so as to let a few Titans pass to Camberwell for a three-bus boost to the 176 upon its extension. Peckham also revised its Mobility Bus routes on 10 September, splitting its 970 to add new variants 971 and 972. On 12 September buses were added to the reawakening Beddington area, which had been treated to an Asda superstore. Routes 254 and 255 were LS-operated by Croydon, linking West Croydon with Wallington and Roundshaw respectively.

In September 1988 Westlink's LS 9 was fitted with the type of shorter-height blinds used in Metroriders and the tops and bottoms of each track's aperture re-masked accordingly; this was in case it needed to turn out on the K3. Fifteen of this unit's LSs were in the new livery by September, plus acquired LS 330, which was the first bus to operate new Surrey County Council contract 568 on 29 October. Between 8 October and 19 November LS 35 from Leyton was loaned to Luton Airport to serve as an airside transfer vehicle, replacing a damage casualty. A loan of LS 35 from Holloway to Harrow Weald in October brought the tapegrey livery briefly back to the 201; after the division of LBL into units, subsequent loans into this operation were from Cricklewood. LS 69 was burnt out on 13 October while working the 126 and withdrawn.

The last LS-operated service at Hornchurch was the 246, and together with the 246A (as 446) it was lost when the garage was closed on 24 September, passing to Ensignbus. One of its National intake was LS 1, newly come in from Red Rover and accepted into the fleet as 502; it was sometimes seen on the 165 as well. The Essex contract 500 was lost to Blue Triangle on 24 October, but another Hertfordshire County Council contract won by LBL from Potters Bar from the 29th was the evening service of the otherwise London Country North East-operated 360 between Waltham Cross and the Rosedale Estate; as well as Ms and Vs, LSs could turn out. Potters Bar took both of the Wood Green LSs on loan during October. Upon its repaint in October LS 438 received a second name; this time it was *City of London*.

On 19 November minibuses came to Peckham; the 70A was sacrificed in favour of new SR-operated P11 and P12. The Ts from the 70, withdrawn at the same time, moved across to the P3 to double-deck it. Rather too long now for its own good, Leyton's 236 was cut in half to terminate at Hackney Wick daily so that new minibus W15 could take over the roads to the north. The redundant stock leaving Leyton, plus several released from Peckham, was stored in the similarly surplus former garage at Hornchurch. AEC's old site played host once again to stored buses, including LSs, during the month.

Although the Bexleybus operation had settled since its unhappy beginning, it was still suffering from chronic staff shortages, and on 19 November two of its LS routes, the 422 and 492, were taken away and given to Boro'Line Maidstone, the next lowest bidder but not by any means without staffing difficulties of its own. Although the majority of the Leyland National complement was composed of ten SNBs hired from London Country North East, four of the LSs sold to Ensign by LBL in the summer found their way to the new operator and popped up on these routes; 901-904, in full Boro'Line livery other than an all-yellow front, were ex-LSs 162, 345, 380 and 436. They also worked in Maidstone, and by the end of 1988 were mostly to be found on the 422, the 492 having been double-decked with ex-Tayside Volvo Ailsas.

The 115 was transferred from Merton to Croydon on the 26th, filling a little space lost by the 157's move away to furnish Suttonbus, but the 152 and 163 were also designated part of this network and moved to Sutton, both gaining DMSs in the process. That marked the official end of LSs at Merton, but LSs 44 and 96 stayed put until 26 January 1989, turning out on the 57 from time to time as emergency cover. All Wandle District LSs were now concentrated at Croydon for what it was worth as the district structure passed out of existence. On 19 November one of the changes in east and

Left: **Comparatively few LSs were bought directly for competitive use against LBL, unlike comparable DMSs, but Boro'Line Maidstone took advantage of Bexleybus's struggles at the end of 1988 to add the 422 and 492 to their already sizeable holdings in that sector. The 492 was supplied with four former LSs purchased from Ensign, and LS 436 at only eight years of age (and with just six of those in service) was a particularly good deal. Last known at Loughton, it became Boro'Line 904 (BYW 436V) and is seen resting at Sidcup Station on 14 August 1989.** *Mike Harris*

Left: **The 200 had struggled in its latter days at Merton and its contract with Cityrama from 22 March 1986 was no different; it was still DMSs, but older and blue. The company decided to cut its losses lest it come to pieces altogether in the manner of Sampson's, and a short-term contract was awarded to the Kingston Bus operation of Norbiton. LSs were made available, helped out by the K10's recently-introduced complement, one of which is LS 165 (THX 165S), managing to take the otherwise long-forgotten Docklands Express livery into 1989.** *Bill Young*

north-east London took the 241 off between Kier Hardie Estate and Canning Town.

For a change, on 3 December a tendered route went the other way, Cityrama surrendering the 200 on its own initiative due to inability to resource it; pending the drafting of a new contract, Norbiton stepped up, using LSs (mostly ex-Peckham plus a couple of Merton's) joined in the peaks by Metrobuses. LS 181 was repainted red with a black skirt during the month, but by the end of 1988 LS 165 was still in Docklands Clipper colours.

The second half of 1988 threw up new rogue LS workings after garages that operated them received allocations on other routes; examples were Leyton LSs on the 48, Bromley LSs on the 208 and Croydon LSs on the 50. Otherwise, Leyton's LS 164 even managed to turn out on the 38 on 25 November, a Wednesday, necessitating a conductor! A first of equal magnitude was West Ham's LS 54 as WH234 on the 8 on Sunday 11 November, although only the number was carried. Not a rogue working but a rogue identity was the appearance of a second 64 at Bexleybus in the form of transferred-in RH 10, which definitely showed both the shortcomings of numeric fleetnumbering and especially when batches allowed no room to slot in extras! Gaps had arisen in the National fleet after the loss of the 422 and 492 prompted the withdrawal of eight LSs, but LS 428 (the true 64) was not among them. In February 1989 it was renumbered 58, assuming the number of LS 284 which had gone to Fulwell Bus Sales.

DECLINING YEARS

s 1988 came to an end, Londoners witnessed the application of unit logos to the LS fleet to underscore the formal division of the five Districts between eleven new wholly-owned subsidiaries of London Buses Ltd. Coming into being on either 7 November (London Central, Selkent) or 5 December (South London, London General, London United, Metroline, London Northern, Leaside Buses, London Forest and East London) and activated officially on 1 April 1989, all of them operated LSs in one capacity or another. Of course, the hassle came when transferred, as buses had to have one logo stripped off and another put on, and the time lag between this actually happening varied sharply. Not a single non-enthusiast passenger noticed, it can be surmised, not even when transfers produced multiple instances of wrongly-branded LSs.

The 398 derived from the 98B; not quite a 'London' bus route but embedded within its territory long years after the overtime ban had forced it to be given away; its present operator Scorpio Coaches now had ex-Bexleybus LS 155 in full blue and cream but with the 'Bexley' removed to read just 'bus'! Ensignbus 502 (LS 1) was hired to Transcity, soon to become an LRT contractor in its own right, to operate the 477 in February 1989 following a fire at its premises, and departed the fleet thereafter. Similarly on the fringes of London were the two LSs with Fountain Coaches of Feltham from February 1989, LSs 282 and 328 (also ex-Bexleybus and retaining those colours) operating a 600 between Bedfont and Hanworth. This route also saw the loan of LS 27 between 12-28 April. One unusual hire between January and around 14 April was of Eastbourne 17, 18, 20, 21 and 22 (formerly

Right: **Boro'Line was to have a sticky end when its reach exceeded its grasp, but at the start of 1989 it was still bedding in on its recently acquired 422 and 492. Five Nationals were hired from Eastbourne Buses between January and April, and all of them were former LSs. Pictured with a compatriot at Boro'Line's Crayford premises during February is 22 (BYW 371V), formerly LS 371 and last working from Bromley.** *Stu Boxall*

LSs 68, 274, 309, 339 and 371) to Boro'Line, which put them out on the 422 in the blue and cream livery that had inspired Bexleybus. The four indigenous ex-LT LSs, meanwhile, could sometimes be seen on the 132, 228 and 328.

Private-hire work was swiftly proving a winner; LSs 173 and 176 were transferred to Wood Green in January to replace the Mark 2s and fitted with tachographs, which didn't stop them going out in normal service when not needed on their contracts; as with the previous two it was on the 221 and 141. The four National 2s on private-hire work, LSs 451

and 489 (having passed from Wood Green to Potters Bar) and LSs 483 and 488 at Holloway, were transferred in February to Walworth for regular Red Arrow work once again, in this case to fulfil the requirement for upcoming new route 505. Only LS 489 was downseated, and LS 491 was fitted with a dot-matrix blind a la LS 268 six years earlier. An obliquely related way of increasing custom was the express route; Norbiton's X71 was introduced on 29 October 1988 with Ms but saw its first LS on 23 January. Chalk Farm was allocated LS 119 in February as the first single-decker to operate from that

Above: **The East London subsidiary logo tops the full LBL tapegrey livery on West Ham's LS 288 (YYE 288T), pulling into East Beckton bus station in April 1989. Treatment of LSs to white-on-black numberplates had largely fallen off by now, but they looked so much smarter while they lasted.**
Haydn Davies

Left: **National 2 LS 489 (GUW 489W) is an unusual sight on the 310A during a crisply cold February 1989 day. It had spent most of its career away from the Red Arrow network, serving variously at Holloway and then Wood Green before pitching up at Potters Bar, but it would return to the Red Arrows shortly after this picture was taken.**
Haydn Davies

garage since 1949; its initial use was on a rail job filling in for rebuilding work at Swiss Cottage station, but they liked what they saw and plans were drawn up to employ more. In March Bromley's LS 393 was fitted with a DAF engine.

On 18 January 1989 a new route was added to the roster operated by Leyton's LSs 105 and 454; this was the 925, making up for the simultaneous withdrawal of the 928. On 1 February the three LSs working the 128 and 128A were stood down after only six months; their replacements were two Leyland Lynxes, LXs 1 and 2 and also owned by the London Borough of Hillingdon. In the same area it now came time for Uxbridge to receive its minibuses, and the first phase of this was on 18 February when the 204 was replaced by new MA-operated U4.

Docklands was growing now at an exponential rate, and already its workforce and population had outpaced the buses provided to the peninsula in the last few years, so they were amended on 4 March. Pioneering route D1 was withdrawn and replaced by three new Titan-operated services (D5, D6 and D7, though West Ham LSs were quickly seen on the D7) which also helped snip the ends off three longer services (5, 106 and 277). The remains of the 8A, operations having latterly been reduced to peak hours only, were withdrawn, but new Red Arrow route 505 from London Bridge to Waterloo combined it with the 5's projections beyond Old Street. Eclipsed by the introduction of minibus-operated W13, the 235 was reduced to a single pair of school journeys and ceded to Eastern National.

22 March saw Nationals appear in force at Chalk Farm, coming out of store at Hornchurch to take over the 168 and much of the 214 from Ts, which were required at Muswell Hill to displace Ms to Potters Bar to see off some Volvo Ailsas. Examples also came from Potters Bar, diminishing the class there after a helpful innings; this year's 318 was accordingly converted to M. LS 112 lost its unique livery for red with a black skirt. Now that they had blind sets including the 17, Holloway's cohort on the 210 spread their wings to that route too. Ensign's lone 502 left the fleet when low-height Bristol VRs were sourced for use on the 246 rather than Nationals, while loans back and forth to Luton Airport over 1989 encompassed LSs 61, 84 and 266. The Autocheck experiment that had also included Bexleybus LSs concluded on 15 April, with the technology, like so many predecessors, not adopted.

On 22 May new Monday to Friday route D4 with West Ham LSs was introduced to link Mile End with Blackwall (Poplar for the first four weeks until roadworks were completed). The second phase of the U-Line scheme at Uxbridge came on 27 May; as well as withdrawing the 224 in favour of new MA-operated U5 and transferring the Uxbridge-Ruislip section of the 223 to new route U1, the plans took the Uxbridge allocation off the 98, together with its leg to Uxbridge station (now the responsibility of new U2). Eight LSs were withdrawn, but until new blinds were printed at Hounslow, the 98 was predominantly M. At Leyton, the 236 was converted from LS to MRL (needing some rerouteing in order to do it) and reallocated

Right: **As the 1980s drew to a close, minibuses started chewing bits off established LS routes as networks based on towns were organised. Just such a move turned the Hillingdon-Uxbridge leg of the 98 over to new MA-operated route U2 on 27 May 1989. Hounslow now operated alone, with LS 124 (THX 124S) seen in August.** *Haydn Davies*

to a reopened Clapton, marking the official end of normal-service LSs at Leyton, though examples lingered until September 1990, making sure to work the 38 (crew and OPO), 48, 55 and 230 before they went. During June the Blackwall Tunnel was closed for maintenance, so at weekends the 108 had to take the long way round via Tower Bridge. And when that was closed on 24 June, it had to go even further, via London Bridge!

An increase to route 258 from 3 June prompted the addition to Harrow Weald of LSs 350 and 354 ex store at Fulwell; while they were being repainted into Harrow Buses livery at Edgware, Cricklewood loaned LS 132 to cover them. 3 June also saw the end of LS operation on the 200 when it passed to the London General subsidiary of LBL and was set going anew with Ms. A former operator of the 200, Merton, however, regained a handful

Above: **LS 119 (THX 119S) was transferred to Chalk Farm in February 1989 but would only spend six months there. It is seen swinging round the war memorial within Euston bus station in June.** *Haydn Davies*

Left: **When it came time to pick the routes that would have to be demoted to single-deck at Chalk Farm to release the Titans needed elsewhere, the 214 proved a sacrifice that could be made without too much trouble, though the similarly backstreet 46 might have been a better choice than the 168. This was before the era of Dart-sized midibuses, which eventually took over the 46 and 214 and have stayed there ever since. However, during the spring of 1989 LS 101 (OJD 901R) is seen at Camden, carrying the London Northern fleetnames appropriate to Chalk Farm's position within LBL's new subsidary organisation.** *Peter Horrex*

Above: **The 283's operation by Scancoaches had been but a blip in the frenzied world of tendering, especially with its unforgettably weird Jonckheere-bodied Scania K92s, but on 1 July 1989 that all ended and LBL resumed control under a three-year contract allocated to Shepherd's Bush. It was not seen fit to restore Ms, however, and seven LSs were collected pending the delivery of new Leyland Lynxes. Without the white band of the new livery but correctly carrying the London United unit logos, LS 138 (THX 138S) is seen in White City during September 1989.**
Haydn Davies

of LSs in June to allow its incumbent DMSs to work the Wimbledon tennis service for 1989 (this year's winners were Boris Becker and Steffi Graf); they worked on the 57 and then left. Another returnee to red buses was the 283 from 1 July, after three years with Scancoaches. Until six new Lynxes were delivered for this further three-year term, LSs 49, 154, 165, 169 and 263 ex-Norbiton and LS 138, 379 and 410 ex-Hounslow were drafted into Shepherd's Bush. But as 1989 continued, the LS was very much on the back foot. StarRiders in particular were the flavour of the month, and on 8 July the 160 and L1 at Catford were converted to SR operation. The B1 lost its roads beyond Eltham to Kidbrooke on the same date so that further SRs could man a B16 linking up severed ends of the B1 and 160, but was extended at the other end to Coney Hall over the 138. On 29 July the sweep of StarRiders through Catford's LS operations continued, taking over the 181 (and 108B on Sundays). The 126 at Bromley once more lost its Eltham-Woolwich projection. Two of the LSs released from Catford, 377 and 386, were put into Bexleyheath, introducing the red livery to that garage but not gaining repaints or local numbers; they made up for the loss of LS 239 (58), written off in a collision. Another July StarRider conversion (to New Cross's 286) had knock-on effects to LSs when the Ts displaced were transferred to Chalk Farm to allow five LSs to leave. LSs 104 and 106 were loaned from Cricklewood to Harrow Weald to cover two accident-damaged Ms, and finally for July

one allocations of LSs came to an end when LS 190, the last at Potters Bar, was delicensed. A first-time appearance was of Cricklewood's LS 394 on the 205 on 21 July. Cricklewood also saw Mobility Bus LS 454 in use between May and July. LS 358 was overhauled by Southend's Tickfield Works in July with the view to contracting out this work, and Luton Airport used LSs 149, 243, 264 and 266 during September.

Almost more a part of Surrey culture than that of London, Westlink helped commemorate the centenary of Surrey County Council in July when it repainted LS 431 in a livery of silver and blue. But bigger things were coming for LBL when, hard on the heels of the successful and popular RMC-operated X15 introduced earlier in the year, it was decided to reseat eighteen LSs (at Hants and Dorset Engineering) and repaint them (at Barking) in a red and gold livery for a second planned incarnation of the D1, intended this time to take higher-spec customers from the rapidly revitalising Docklands office-block cluster to the City and Waterloo. Still further special repaints put ex-London Coaches LS 27, now at Muswell Hill for similar private-hire work to that at Wood Green, into red with a white flash tapering down to the front and shortly afterwards, 'Muswell Hill' in stylised white Gothic script on a black base across the front. Similarly single-doored special LS 76, once of Wandsworth, was now at Holloway and appearing on the 210. Wood Green's LS 173 was itself keeping busy with debut visits to the

W2 and then the 41, and, with recently-acquired partner LS 176, turning out at weekends for Enfield's Saturday trips to Southend. By September Westlink's repaint programme was now complete, but not far away, Norbiton's LSs 57 and 130 found themselves repainted with blue bumpers! Despite its repaint out of Docklands Clipper livery earlier in the year, LS 181 at the same garage managed to retain the red entrance doors and white exit doors of that scheme.

The 108 was about to depart LBL for Boro'Line Maidstone, but this was postponed and on 19 August it struck up a temporary contract with East London, i.e. with its existing West Ham LSs. Bromley's peripatetic 471 was ceded to Kentish Bus. In September Hornchurch garage was obliged to cease its use as a storage facility and eleven LSs lodged there were sold.

September saw the placing into use of six LSs refurbished for a government training scheme; LSs 60, 83 and 111 were based at Chalk Farm (with LS 144 in reserve), LS 44 at Camberwell as a seat store and LS 86 at Merton. With a small number of LSs still based at Leyton, the garage took on loan wheelchair-accessible KEP 829X, a National 2 of South Wales Transport during September and used it on the 230 in the interests of future accessibility legislation and with Leyton's Mobility Bus experience in mind; the bus (named *Sir Harry Secombe*) had also spent time at Kentish Bus's Dunton Green garage.

On 11 September the 283 took charge of its new Lynxes, although LS 165 stayed put just in case; the stopgap LSs returned to Norbiton. The Cargo Tunnel at Heathrow was closed to buses on 30 September, thus cutting off Heathrow Bus Station from Terminal 4 unless a very long detour was attempted; other than in the case of the 285 it wasn't, from either direction, and for LSs' purposes the 202 now finished at Terminal 4. 28 October saw the 214 (but not the 168) regain full T operation and further changes

Above: **Harrow Weald's LS fleet often needed the benefit of loans from Cricklewood, but that garage's own Nationals remained in LBL fleet livery and thus took it to the 201, as LS 106 (OJD 906R) is doing in August 1989. This particular repaint hasn't seen fit to include the bumper.** *Haydn Davies*

applied to the Red Arrows. The 506 and 509 were withdrawn but the 510 was extended from Aldgate to Liverpool Street and the 503 rerouted to Bloomsbury and (on Mondays to Fridays) extended on from there to Moorgate. Finally Westlink won Surrey tenders to use their Hounslow Heath LSs on routes 501, 536, 566, 567 and 569.

Bexleybus's double-deck fleet was changing rapidly in the autumn as Titans flooded in to replace the worst of the DMSs, but the LSs stayed stable; although LSs 377 and 386 departed, LS 17 was another red one into Bexleyheath, albeit wearing London Forest logos and London Northern legals! The existing fleet was considered extremely rough

Right: **The Red Arrow network had never been particularly successful away from its Victoria, Waterloo and London Bridge cores; an attempt to serve Paddington instead of RM-operated 36A lasted little more than a year, and in June 1989 on the 506 LS 457 (GUW 457W) isn't carrying a full load round Marble Arch.** *Haydn Davies*

THE LONDON LS

by now and in desperate need of replacement, but the dribs and drabs of surplus LSs put in over the cusp of 1989/90 weren't much better, with 'alien' unit names and legals and bits of cardboard serving as blinds. At Bromley, LS 382 as TB163 was a debut appearance on the 1 on 16 October; stablemate LS 26 was damaged in a collision with a dustcart on the 21st and wasn't deemed repairable. Among the eight Nationals sold in October 1989 were LSs 192, 202 and 290, the three hitherto unused Mobility Bus conversions, but they wouldn't be forgotten quite yet as, still owned by LRT, they were allocated to Kentish Bus for use in the New Year. Boro'Line was set to pick up LS 287 in July but the sale was cancelled.

As repaints into gold-accented red for the putative D1 continued to the end of the year, the LSs affected were allocated to West Ham, directly replacing existing examples for withdrawal but not yet entering service. Muswell Hill used its customised LS 27 on a new Christmas service (611) linking Wood Green and Brent Cross between 4 November and 9 December, and on the 25th (till 23 December) Holloway added a 610 from the Angel, using single-doored LS 76. On 25 November the 108 passed from West Ham to Boro'Line as planned, and that was the decade. 1989 closed out with another 38 LSs sold.

1990 started with a programme on 6 January whereby, among other changes, the 115 at Croydon was augmented and converted from LS to MR minibus operation. This wasn't the only loss to Nationals at that garages, as eight were replaced by Ls cascaded from Streatham following their own replacement by Ms. What LSs remained on the 166 saw their own route hacked in half, the roads east of Shirley passing to a new minibus pair numbered 366 and 367.

The reduced complement at Croydon still came in useful, however, as following the storm of 25 January they were put out on the 130 in lieu of the existing DMSs and Ls, just to be on the safe side; one even turned out on the 403, assumed in stages from London & Country at the end of the previous year.

Shepherd's Bush had kept a lone LS (165) as backup to the Lynxes since their arrival, but with the transfer of the 283 to Stamford Brook on 6 January, lost it; on the day before the change Hounslow lent LS 138. The simultaneous arrival of new Ls on the 237 cascaded Stamford Brook's Ms to Norbiton to see off not only most of its DMSs, but five LSs too.

Below: **For many years a solid connection from south of Croydon to points east of Croydon, the 166 nonetheless was on the lower rung of importance when it came to allocating vehicles, and thus spent the latter end of the 1980s as a LS operation. As 1990 opened it was cut in half and its roads to Beckenham Junction minibussed. LS 237 (THX 237S), based at Croydon since February 1987, was repainted into tapegrey in February 1989 and is seen at Croydon flyover shortly before moving to Kingston on 29 September 1990.** *Tom Gurney*

If 1989 was the year of the StarRider, 1990 was dominated by the cheaper and distinctly nastier Renault 50, which with a Reeve Burgess body was known as the RB class, and on 24 February the S2 lost its LSs in favour of these vehicles, transferring from West Ham to Bow in the process. This was the day the gold-banded LSs at West Ham, still waiting for the green light on their intended D1, first saw service with two on the 299. The fleet eventually comprised eleven (LSs 7, 35, 88, 97, 123, 177, 227, 245, 259, 395 and 411), but there was a problem; the East London unit had got ahead of itself by doing up buses for a route that was subsequently submitted to tender and awarded to the London Forest unit with Titans. Chalk Farm was able to shed two LSs when six Titans came in from Leyton, but the LS wasn't done yet here. At Leyton itself, three years after the Forester route had been consigned to history, LS 71 was finally repainted, but this time into a further custom livery of red with white band and red stripe within it. On 24 March, once further but slow-arriving RBs were all delivered, the 276 also underwent transfer from West Ham to Bow and conversion from LS. However, even with the transfer of two RWs from the impending Ealing operation to help out, West Ham was called upon to offer assistance with its own LSs and all appeared as it had been for a little longer.

Miscellany for the start of 1990 saw Bexleybus LSs, among the unit's other vehicles bar the outgoing DMSs, gaining their proper 'London Transport' fleetnumbers on the front and back to accompany those already on the sides; LS 389 (Bexleybus 63) was not included due to being hit up the rear in Thamesmead on 27 February and withdrawn. New oddments were both from Hounslow, which proceeded to stick an LS out on the E4 and 27 for the first time on each in the last week of February. At Cricklewood, LSs continued to drift from the 245 to the 32 and Harrow Weald's to the 114 (for old times' sake), 140 and 183. Eighteen months after losing the main routes they worked on, Peckham could still muster a number of LSs as spare cover, putting them out on the 78 from time to time. Sales of the class were now picking up in earnest as minibuses, love them or hate them, continued to gather on their traditional and latter-day routes.

The LS was definitely in its twilight now; fifteen came off with the loss of the 276 and, as double-deckers became available, they were used to winnow down strongholds like Bromley, which took on two, delicensed four more and added six Titans to use mostly on the 126. Confidence in newer generations led to longstanding spare allocations being stood down, LS 240 of the standby Hillingdon LSs

going for scrap in January and LSs 222 and 236 being sold in March. The scrapyard, specifically the infamous PVS premises at Barnsley and Trevor Wigley's facilities next door, was now an increasingly prevalent initial destination for sold LSs.

On 26 March Kentish Bus began a series of nine Mobility Bus routes (911-919) using the three LSs supplied to them by LRT the previous October. Retaining their fleetnumbers, without any parallel Kentish Bus identities at this point, LSs 192, 202 and 290 operated out of Northfleet, some distance from the routes'

epicentre at Croydon. Westlink LSs (or the supporting BL they had at the time) took over the collapsed Fountain Coaches' pair of routes on contract to Surrey County Council on 7 April; these were the 600 and 602. A week later came the usual summer Sunday extensions of the 116 and 216 from Staines to Thorpe Park; despite all the upheaval that had gone on, these could be relied upon to stay much the same. Westlink's acquisition of the 110 from London & Country was carried out with new Optare Deltas, but LSs could soon be counted on to stand in where needed. LSs 173 and 176,

the coach-seated Leaside Buses private-hire vehicles (capacity now DP44F+14 following their concurrent conversion to single-door), were finally deployed to Enfield and set to work on the Southend run, prohibited to Ms since a deroofing to one of them.

The set of routes into and out of the Isle of Dogs were revised again on 21 April; this time the 5 was restored to most of its old roads and the D5 reduced to an LS-operated service from West Ham on Mondays to Friday daytimes only, using the coach-seated LSs intended for the D1 had East London won it. Despite its now limited spectrum, the D5 was marketed as 'The Docklands Shuttle' to make use of the already

applied gold branding. The D4 was withdrawn at the same time, but not before also having seen some of the red and gold LSs that became the only such examples at West Ham after the rest were cleared out following the programme. From time to time they were turned out on the 299 and D6, and LS 7 was adopted as the latter-day garage showbus.

If the Leyland National exemplified the ethos of standardisation, the Dennis Dart was its polar opposite, its chassis (in three lengths) available for bodying by anyone who fancied it, but to a smaller footprint with consequent weight and fuel savings. It was these that really put an end to the LS after an adequate and broadly trouble-

THE LONDON LS

free decade in service. Duple (later Carlyle) bodied LBL's first 8.5m examples as the DT class during 1990, fulfilling the London United subsidiary's tendering victories implemented in the spring. One of their first deployments was on the H22, the replacement for the 202 from 28 April. Six Hounslow LSs were withdrawn, leaving a small number meant for the 98, but naturally they soon racked up appearances on all three of the new routes, H21, H22 and H23, as well as regular wanderings to the 232 and E4. Their last target was the 91, and this was accomplished on 4 June in the form of LS 138 as AV10. New visits for this portion of 1990 comprised Croydon's route 12A/12B-based LSs on the 166 and recently-introduced minibus route 366 (the latter of which had a scheduled double-deck working that proved fair game for LSs), plus Leyton LSs on the 257. Cricklewood loaned a pair of LSs to Harrow Weald on a regular basis, LSs 104 and 106 in this role being replaced in June by LSs 70 and 363. They kept the standard tapegrey alive at Harrow Weald, as did LSs 218 and 386 at Bexleyheath in a sea of blue and white, though LS 218 retained Centrewest fleetnames (and a most non-standard black roof pod!). Summer-season London Zoo route Z1, the responsibility of Chalk Farm, was visited by ex-London Coaches LS 30 (which could also be found on the 168 despite the further depletion of that garage's LS fleet in May). Transferred to Enfield, LSs 173 and 176 (now with underlined front fleetnames and a pair of white bands above and below the headlights) eked out their private-hire work with visits to the 144A, recently transferred in part from Wood Green but suffering a shortage

of Ms, and shortly after that, the 121 and 191. LS 173 suffered accident damage on 25 August and was sent for prolonged repair. But June saw the elimination of non-Mobility Bus LSs from Peckham, LSs 58, 201, 300, 403 and 413 being withdrawn without replacement.

On 14 July Bromley's LS route B1 met its end, reconfigured as DT/MRL-operated 314. A second stage to this Bromley minibus scheme cost the 126 its LSs on 11 August in favour of the same combination, and rendered the 227 the only remaining LS route at Bromley (though visits to the 1 and particularly the 119 remained common, at the same time as the new Darts and Metroriders were encroaching upon the 227). The 21 July changes surrounding the closure of Muswell Hill saw LS 360 put into Potters Bar, returning the class if by just one; it was used on the W8. Special-purposes LS 27 also made the move. Special purposes also surrounded the transfer of LSs 79 and 413 to Stamford Brook, where they were added to the Airbus services in July after an Underground closure forced passengers onto the A1 and A2. LS 413 was further devolved, between 27 October and 23 November, to a service linking Belgravia hotels to Grosvenor Gardens where they could board the regular services; for this purpose it had ten seats replaced by luggage racks (rendering its capacity DP43F). Further south, Westlink's BL 81 failed not long after assuming route 592 and LSs took over until its water pump was repaired.

During this year's Farnborough Air Show LSs furnished an internal shuttle, using five from West Ham and seven from Croydon. A new contractor was in evidence when LSs 121

Right: **Croydon's LS 114 (THX 114S) looks smart other than the paint flaking off its bumper. This March 1990 shot sees the 12A with six months to go before the replacement of its core route by new double-deck route 312 and the concurrent turning over of its quieter end to a Dart-operated series numbered 412.** *Haydn Davies*

and 403 were converted for wheelchair use by East Midland, and a surprise was thrown up when the third National to be treated by this concern wasn't an original LS at all but ex-Southdown 65, which was taken into LBL stock as LSL 1. On 4 August the K10 at Norbiton was withdrawn, but the garage's LSs proved stubborn to leave and LS 130 made a final trip to the 85 on 18 September, eleven days before that route's loss to London & Country.

On 25 August (but in practice a week earlier) the D6 at Ash Grove was converted from T to LS, ironically so that Titans could be provided for the D1 starting after the Bank Holiday. Ash

Grove had already taken in LSs for a school contract during July. Three more came from Leyton, which received some Ash Grove Ts on loan in exchange, followed by five from store at Fulwell. West Ham was the recipient of four LSs replaced at Bromley when the B1 was lost, and on 30 August one of the longer-established LS services came to an end. The offending bridge that had prohibited double-deckers on the 12A (and its Sunday counterpart 12B) was now removed, and the routes were recast as daily L-operated 312. Underscoring the nominal exit of LSs from Croydon, the 254/255 pair were consolidated as 255 only and double-decked. But after 1 September only seven LSs (117, 226, 323, 332, 333, 343 and 409) remained at Croydon, turning out on the 166 and 194 (with one most unusual loan of LS 254 to Thornton Heath on the 12th and 20th to work new route 412 (the sleepier southern end of the old 12A) as TH254). LSs 108 and 160 were added in November.

Two outermost non-London Transport operators were fielding Nationals in 1990; one shadowing route 109 in the form of Panther Travel, which counted among its fleet LS 180, 188, 230, 313 and 322, and one (Blue Triangle) with bona fide ex-LBL LSs 113, 174 and 300 on its 265. Panther went out of business on 2 January 1992 and its fleet was repossessed.

Westlink's LSs remained perennial examples of the Leyland National within London, and on 5 September they struck up a new allocation on new schoolday-only route 213S, which added a Ham leg to the normal 213 as far as New Malden. On 22 September a couple of new Saturday-only Mobility Bus routes (920 and 929) were added to Leyton's roster, replacing the 923's service

Below: **Ash Grove's LS 413 (BYW 413V) can only muster a cut-up Titan blind when captured in September 1990 after the single-decking of the D6, so for added reassurance a slipboard (and probably another panel repurposed from a Titan) is carried.** *Haydn Davies*

on that day of the week. Leyton's non-Mobility handful continued to operate on the 230 and 257. On the same day two more garage's LSs departed on 22 September when Chalk Farm's 168 and Holloway's 210 were both lost to Grey-Green; or so it was intended, anyway, as four LSs (30, 89, 160 and 388) remained at Chalk Farm as spare buses (turning out on the 46) and three (LSs 311, 360 and 415) at Holloway (visiting the 17). Potters Bar's lone LS 360 left that garage at this point, albeit passing to Holloway to see the class out in January.

Kingston Bus's unhappy story ended on 29 September after three years, with the LSs already gone from Norbiton and thus no further possibilities. New route 371, however, which took over the 71's northern end, was commenced with Westlink LSs out of Kingston until its new DWL-class Dennis Darts were

delivered. Sixteen were put into Kingston, all but two of them coming from Croydon, and almost immediately spread to the 131, acquired at the same time with Titans. Westlink's 600 came off so that LRT tenders H24 and H25 could take over, operated for the moment by Hounslow MRs (with, naturally, one LS wandering to the H24 as early as 10 October).

On 6 October the D3 was extended from Plaistow, Greengate to East Ham in support of the 5, with the short 299 coming off, and on the 27th a spread of eleven more Mobility Bus routes (951-961) was introduced, awarded to the East London unit of LBL for operation out of North Street. LSs 121 and 403, plus LS 105 transferred from Leyton (making two in service plus one spare) were transferred in ownership from LBL to LRT, on the model of the Kentish Bus Mobility Bus operations. LSL

Left: **Passengers' north-south path across Kingston was definitively severed on 29 September 1990 when the 71 was curtailed from the south and the leg onwards via Ham to Richmond converted to single-deck as new route 371. Darts were ordered and on the way, but until then the trusty LSs would do just fine. Coming into Kingston town centre is LS 267 (THX 267S), transferred from Croydon to Kingston and destined for sale once the loan period was up. The Titan it is passing on the 131, won by Westlink at the same time, was evidence of changing times, as the type was unknown in this part of town.** *Colin Lloyd*

Left: **Rather more luxury than was carried on your usual LS is in evidence thanks to the coach seats fitted to LS 403 (BYW 403V) in time for it to take over a batch of Mobility Bus routes operated by North Street. The twelve services commenced on 27 September and the bus is pictured in Romford during the ensuing month.** *Haydn Davies*

Right: **Airbus had gone from strength to strength since its introduction in 1980, the main component being on its second generation of purpose-built Metrobuses by the end of the decade. Thoughts toward expansion ran as to how to get the airport passengers and their luggage closer to the hotels they would be staying at, and to this end LS 435 (BYW 435V), already single-doored and to a dual-purpose spec from its time on the X99 and then at London Coaches, was put to work on a route that would take Pimlico-area hotel guests to Victoria, where they could board the A1. Not long after its reassignment to this work, it is seen in Buckingham Palace Road.** *Colin Lloyd*

1 took LS 105's place at Leyton. The 28th also saw Walworth closed once again so that its Red Arrow routes (501, 502, 503, 505, 507, 510 and 513) could move into their new purpose-built premises on the site of the old Cornwall Road bus stand adjacent to Waterloo Station. Finally for this date, Airbus LS 435 was put to work on a free shuttle linking Pimlico hotels to the Victoria pick-up point of the A1; it was downseated to DP32F to accommodate extra luggage space. The other high-end LS at Stamford Brook, LS 79, wandered to the 237 on 1 September and by November it had received Airbus Shuttle

signwriting in time to make a return voyage to the 283; it retained its full complement of seating. LS 71 at Leyton, meanwhile, finally lost its Forester livery, gaining a new scheme of red with a white-red-white stripe that stepped down to bumper level. It was put to work on a new commercial shoppers' service X10, operating three times a week until Christmas from north-east London pick-up points to Southend. LS 275 was the usual backup bus.

After three years with LSs obliged by the need to divert Ms elsewhere, the 245 at Cricklewood was converted back to M on 17

Right: **Ever since the 119 had been converted to OPO, Bromley had put its LSs out on it. LS 265 (THX 265S) is doing just that when seen in July 1990, shortly prior to its own withdrawal.**
Haydn Davies

November, removing the type here other than the three Mobility Bus examples. Three of them were put into Harrow Weald to replace a pair of accident victims there for the last two months of the Harrow Buses adventure. The 24th saw Bexleybus's operation transferred wholesale from Selkent to London Central within LBL, including Bexleyheath garage; this was in advance of the tender changes on 19 February that would otherwise finish off this often ill-starred operation. Boro'Line's four LSs were on borrowed time, but remained to work the 492 alone following the double-decking of the 422.

Another loss to LSs came in the withdrawal of the 98 on 1 December so that new DT-operated H98 could take over. A week later, the 371 at Westlink's Kingston received its DWLs, although a lone school journey in each peak from Richmond to and from Ham was diagrammed for an LS. Croydon could still muster a handful of LSs, but during December loaned seven of them to Streatham, the latest operator of the 115, to fill in for Metroriders.

149 LSs were sold in 1990, over a third of the number of Mark Is delivered. Most sales by the beginning of 1991 were directly to the scrapyard before interest in them picked up again mid-year. One last hurrah for a once long-established LS route saw Leyton put LS 275 out on the N96 on New Year's Eve. 1991 otherwise began with only penny numbers of the surviving LSs not in tapegrey, with Westlink ploughing its own furrow and the Bexleybus and Harrow Buses identities about to breathe their last. On 14 January the 213S at Westlink's Kingston was converted from LS to DWL operation. At this point LS 195 was fitted with a DAF engine.

Above: **When not employed on the Mobility Bus services, LSL 1 (WYJ 165S) was put to work on rail replacements, like this one covering the Central Line to Liverpool Street.** *Colin Lloyd*

Bexleybus came to an end on 19 January upon the award of very nearly all of its services to other operators. For LSs' purposes, the 244 and 269 were two of them, the former (under London Central) taking MRLs and the latter going to Kentish Bus. Five Bexleybus-liveried LSs lingered, including red LS 218, which had not only received a Bexleybus fleetname in red but never lost the Centrewest one it was transferred in with, but within a month their numbers were reduced to just LSs 28, 135 and 218 and they were all gone by March. The first and last LS route at Bromley, the 227, had its

Left: **Everything looks calm enough for a well-loaded LS 434 (BYW 434V) at Feltham in September 1989, but Westlink was about to face a threat to its operation when all three of its routes came up for tender.** *Haydn Davies*

Sunday service converted to DT and MRL operation, and finally Boro'Line stood down its four ex-LT LSs, moving them onto its core operations in Maidstone. At Harrow Weald, the similarly ill-starred tendering network there was also finished off on 19 January, new contracts seeing the withdrawal of both the leased and second-hand double-deckers but also of the LSs when the 201 was recast as new Sovereign-operated route H10. Rather than close Harrow Weald, it was decided to reduce Cricklewood's operations substantially and as part of associated transfers the Mobility Bus routes 981-989, plus their LSs, passed to Harrow Weald.

The two LSs at Stamford Brook had now lost their Airbus Direct augmentation and from 23 February (between continued visits to the 237 and 283) began helping out on new LX-operated route 190, which took over from the DT-converted 283. LS 435 had the seats it had lost during its Airbus Direct days refitted for the purpose. Hounslow's LSs now appeared on absolutely anything based there; even the N11 on 10 February! The admirable (if maddening to catch and photograph) flexibility continued when LS 324 subbed a stricken M as AV310 on the recently acquired 140 on 27 March.

On 4 March the Kentish Bus-operated Croydon-area Mobility Bus network added a route 930. Extensive changes to routes in south-east London on 27 April cost the 227 its Bromley North-Chislehurst section; five Bromley LSs found themselves withdrawn. The 1 was removed from consideration for LSs with its retraction out of the area and concurrent removal of the Bromley allocation. During April the 213S at Westlink effectively resumed LS operation; the LSs were rarer on the 131 but still very much in evidence.

Then there was the Wandsworth Area Scheme on 25 May. One such new route was the H37 at Hounslow, taking over its former route 37 allocation as a DR/DT operation, but the garage's LSs quickly added it to their repertoire through two scheduled 'big bus' journeys. Since the new route went under the low bridge at Isleworth rather than skirt it as did the old 37, that was the best that could be done. With very few permanent or complete LS allocations left by now, there remained the stable Red Arrow fleet, but even this declined with the withdrawal of routes 503 and 510,

though a new 511 was introduced to take over the Victoria Waterloo section of the C1. Nine LSs were taken out of service and put in store at Fulwell, but their careers, unlike most Mark 1 LSs at this point, were far from over quite yet as two of them gathered at Uxbridge, to be followed over the next few weeks by the rest. Following an eye-opening visit of LS 117 to the 68 on 20 May and another loan of a Croydon LS to Thornton Heath for backup on the 412, June finally saw the last two at Croydon, LSs 160 and 343, taken out of service. On 29 June the D3's Saturday service was converted from T to LS, the previous few Saturdays already having seen partial or total LS operation. Schools service 338 had been inaugurated with Bromley Titans, but on 30 April an LS was seen, having brought itself across on the TB31 duty linked from the 119.

Even Westlink's bread and butter was as vulnerable to the vicissitudes of tendering by now as were the routes of any other operator, LBL-derived or independent, and on 10 August this company lost its entire LRT portfolio out of Hounslow Heath. The 116 and 117 passed to Tellings-Golden Miller and the 203 to London Buslines, but by some adroit manoeuvring (specifically the introduction of a commercial route 417 paralleling much of the 117), Westlink was able to keep Hounslow Heath open. And on 31 August its Kingston LSs commenced new route 468 (formerly Surrey County Council

contract 568) across the Chessington peninsula into Epsom. Surrey County Council contracts 572 and 582 replaced the 216 on Sundays (with the rest of that route transferring from Kingston to Hounslow Heath), a similar new 578 served for the Sunday service on London & Country's 479 and the 213S was withdrawn. LS 30 was repainted into Westlink livery and put to use as the replacement for BL 81 on the 592.

Despite the encroachment of minibuses onto Mobility Bus services when new tenders were drawn up, the National was not quite done here; indeed during June another long-wheelbase example was acquired from Southdown (ex-42) and became LSL 2. Its stablemate (43) was also pencilled in for acquisition as LSL 3 but the order was cancelled and ended up scrapped. Post-conversion (by East Midland at Chesterfield, LSL 2 was allocated to Kentish Bus at Northfleet to increase capacity on the popular Croydon-area network, which on 13 July added a new route 934. LS 290 passed to Leyton, but was back at Northfleet in September.

During August the first of the ex-Red Arrow National 2s into Uxbridge commenced work on the U1, which was extended from Ruislip to Uxbridge over the withdrawn 128 and acquired some 'big bus' journeys in addition to the normal runout of MA-class Mercedes 811Ds. LS 484 was the first converted to single-door for the purpose, but the whole intake (plus the two LXs made redundant from the 128 at the

Above: **On 23 September 1991 the D3 at West Ham was demoted to LS from Titan so that the Ts could supply three new Docklands Light Railway fill-ins. Here at Limehouse is LS 160 (THX 160S), taken out of store after last working from Croydon. Amazingly, this was its third separate tour of duty at West Ham, having worked from there between September 1982 and October 1984 and then between October 1986 and April 1989. This shuffling of progressively older and older vehicles couldn't last, and finally the East London subsidiary put its hand in its pocket and bought some new double-deckers in the form of Scanias.** *Colin Lloyd*

same time) was intended for the conversion of the 607 imminently and conversions to coach spec with high-backed blue seating were ongoing throughout the late summer and into the autumn. Due to the withdrawal of the rest, these were the only LSs in original form to receive the full DiPTAC treatment mandated by recent legislation, to wit receiving high-visibility coats of paint on the handrails (in this case they were green) and fluorescent yellow/black sawtooth strips on the step edges. LS 173, restored to service at Enfield in August (using parts ex-West Ham LSs) after a long spell out of service, received the green handrails but no more than that. It continued to see service on

the 144A (blinded as 144), 191 and 121. The plan was for the 144A to shed its suffix upon the concurrent renumbering of the existing 144 to 444, but that didn't end up happening.

In the autumn of the original LSs' career came another conversion on 23 September when the rest of the D3 gained LSs, namely eleven tired-looking ones from store plus LS 27; the existing Ts were needed to furnish three new permanent routes shadowing the Docklands Light Railway replacement work and such a move was more efficient than having to keep borrowing adjacent garages' Titans every weekend. Slipboards had to be carried in the absence of destination blinds. For the National

Right: **Speeding west past Bushy Park in January 1990 is Kingston's LS 431 (BYW 431V), painted silver during the previous year to celebrate the centenary of Surrey County Council. It lasted in this scheme until July 1993, and much later was one of the Urban Bus conversions that saw out LS operations with Hounslow.** *Haydn Davies*

2s, however, a new and prestige gig was about to unfold; in concert with Lynxes, all but two of full complement of LSs 444, 451, 458, 470, 472, 484, 495, 497, 503 and 504, repainted with black window surrounds and given route branding, implemented the conversion of the 607 on 16 November. To provide the panels for the single-door conversions, accident-damaged former Solent Blue Line 432 (JTH 754P) was purchased and stripped. Naturally, since the LSs were fitted with blind sets including the 222 and 223, they made sure to pay visits to those routes as fit. LSs 495 and 472 were the last to be done, the last one entering service in April.

One of the many options for Hounslow's LSs fell away on 9 November with the renumbering of the E4 to H40 and its relaunch as a minibus route. That was the same day the 27 assumed a new contract with just London United of LBL, the London Northern aspect operated by Holloway coming off and the whole going into Stamford Brook (where it now terminated). The H37's scheduled LS journeys were also reduced in scope as further new DRs arrived, but the type continued to wander to this and everything else at Hounslow (barring the 9 on Sundays).

Perhaps the last regular repaint, even with only months left for it, was of Bromley's LS 91 in October 1991. In the same month Westlink's LS 363 was repainted and signwriting added advertising training to join the company. At almost the close of regular LS operation, Hounslow, which had set the ball rolling, adapted the blinds of two more modern types to go in the rear of two of their Nationals, LS 57

receiving a set of rollers out of a DT and LS 389 a one-piece MM number box out of a Metrobus.

Chalk Farm's LS assistance had held out for more than a year after the loss of their official routes, but upon the conversion of the 46 from T to SR on 9 November they couldn't stay any more and departed. Customised LS 27 was the last, and it was quickly plucked from store at Fulwell to join the fleet at West Ham. On 23 November the LS routes in the Isle of Dogs and based on Stratford were swapped to reflect changing requirements upon the deletion of London Forest and concurrent closure of Ash Grove. This garage passed the D6 to West Ham on Mondays to Fridays and to Bow on Saturdays, converting it from LS to T; West Ham's existing D5 also regained the double-deckers. To release them, the 241 and 278 were demoted to LS operation on Mondays to Saturdays, but both were already intended for minibuses and MRLs took over three days later. The D3's cross-Docklands remit was revised to take off the Old Street leg and reroute it into the peninsula from the east. West Ham's gold-banded LSs, though reduced in number by twelve, stayed put on this route alone, though in customary fashion continued to wander to the 241, 262, 278, D3, D5 and D7.

Finally for what was one of the most extensive set of transfers in recent London bus history, the Mobility Bus routes based at Leyton were split between two garages. The 900, 901, 906-910, 920, 947, 948, 966 and 973 were reallocated to North Street, taking LS 396 with them to pool with the existing ones. LSs 356 and 454, however, passed to Clapton for the 921-925, 927 and 929.

Above: **Bromley's LS 91 (OJD 891R) was the last LS to undergo a repaint, and in its last spell on the 227 is seen at Beckenham Junction.** *Tom Gurney*

As 1992 opened, the LS in 'London Transport' was almost done (97 of them having been sold in 1991), but in a period of deep recession compounded by the severe effects wrought on the bus industry by deregulation and privatisation, an ethos of 'make do and mend' came to the fore again. This took the humble but ageing Leyland National and transformed it at the hands of East Lancs into a modern, re-engined and repanelled citybus at a fraction of the cost of buying new. LS 466 was the pilot example of the Greenway project, having been sent for conversion in November 1991 specifying the new front and rear designed by

Best Impressions, but both this and the other guinea pig, a second-hand purchase, were not taken into stock until October 1992. The treatment included a Gardner engine and ZF gearbox; the roof pod came off at last and a KL convector unit provided heat. Inside, there was Transmatic lighting.

LSs 173 and 176 were withdrawn from Enfield in January, their eclectic work being deemed superfluous upon the impending mass recasting of routes there on 1 February. Talk about eclectic; the first re-registration of an LS came in January when Uxbridge's LS 503 received 503 CLT off departing RMC 1503. Re-registrations had become a popular craze over the past four years but none had as yet accrued to an LS; in the end twelve of the class (in either LS or the later GLS form) would be done, plus the lone acquired Greenway. Westlink was committed to the LS in the long term, however, and nine of their existing fleet were withdrawn in January in preparation for replacement by higher-spec ones, including several earmarked from the numbers still in service at West Ham and in fact transferred in ownership to Stanwell Buses. West Ham wasn't giving them up just yet, however, in fact taking back all its most recently withdrawn examples as the D6 reverted to LS on 1 February 1992 due to the need for Titans to be cascaded to Catford for the 36B prior to its OPO conversion on 14 March.

LS 270 was sent to Romania on an aid mission during March, then was sold upon its return. Two arguably weirder trips were of Mobility Bus LS 105 to the 345 as NS452 on 27 January 1992, and of a Kingston LS to the 371S on the 5th.

Right: **Working through Fleet Street as Christmas 1992 approaches is GLS 1 (GUW 466W), herald of a brave new world for the Red Arrow routes.** *Tony Wilson*

On 29 February LS operation at Bromley came to an end with the exit of its first such route, the 227, which passed to Kentish Bus. LSs 90, 91, 204, 216, 291, 348, 349, 366, 367, 382, 406 and 412 were the last twelve remaining and LS 216, duplicated by RF 383, was the last in service on the 28th. National operation continued, but these were 'SNBs' and thus out of the scope of this book; and would be even more so when they went in for conversion to Greenway specification by East Lancs and came out with different faces and different fleetnumbers. Bromley's long-running LSs having come off, now Hounslow's followed suit when LS 57 was delicensed during March.

This bus had been fitted latterly with the rear blind box out of a DT. Although, as it turned out, this wouldn't be the last this garage saw of the type, their innings there had marked nearly sixteen years. Hounslow turned out to be the penultimate LS operator outside Westlink, as West Ham lost another LS operation on 9 May with the cession of the D6 to Capital Citybus, losing all but LS 395. The D5 could now regain Ts, and West Ham thus lost its fleet, which at the end comprised LSs 7, 20, 27, 35, 58, 65, 71, 97, 108, 123, 160, 177, 191, 218, 245, 334 and 407. Only LS 395 remained, being kept as a spare until June. That marked the end of original Leyland National operations by LBL.

The Mobility Bus routes continued on, though this dignified and stress-free work had bought the LSs so employed a considerable extension of their lifespans. Repaints to the Peckham examples encompassed LS 320 in March, LS 293 in April and LS 139 in May, and on 1 June the Croydon-area routes operated by Kentish Bus dropped the 914 and gained a new 926 and 928. The 915 was the busiest, requiring the extra capacity of regular runner LSL 2, but between 27 April and the end of May LS 403 was loaned from North Street to allow the main three to undergo modifications. Both the North Street and the Clapton operations had now been tendered, and on 20 June passed to Capital Citybus on a two-year contract, taking the four buses with them to Northumberland Park. LSs 356, 396, 454 and LSL 1 thus became 795, 796, 794 and 797 in that order and gained yellow bands over their otherwise still red livery. Kentish Bus's LS 192 was returned to LBL in August and then sold to Northumbria for continued use as a wheelchair-accessible bus, bringing the concept to Newcastle.

Now, other than the commercial operations of Westlink, the two Stamford Brook LSs 79 and 435 filling in where needed (having lost their Airbus livery for corporate during March and LS 79 receiving a single-track blind) and the upgraded LSs on the 607, all that was left were the Red Arrow National 2s. On 18 May the 502 and 513 were fused into new route 521, and in order to permit the Waterloo base to close at weekends and thus not disturb the residents any more than was felt it had been doing already, the 507 was passed on Saturdays and Sundays to Victoria's basement and converted to SR. Nine LSs were delicensed; some of them were seconded to Stockwell in August for Farnborough Air Show shuttle work, following on from similar specialist use at Putney affecting LSs 485 and 486 between May and July.

Below: **In the question of which way it was more useful to route Red Arrow passengers coming from London Bridge into the City, the decision was made that this was via Cannon Street rather than Bank; accordingly, from 18 May 1992 the 502 and 513 were withdrawn and their remit combined into new route 521. LS 446 crosses London Bridge in September.** *Haydn Davies*

Above: **Uxbridge's LS 504 (GUW 504W) illustrates the full route 607 specification, with coach seats in blue moquette, single-door conversion and copious but discreet route branding. The bus is full to bursting as it thunders westward along the Uxbridge Road during August 1992, underscoring the 607's great success.** *Haydn Davies*

Westlink's Surrey contracts changed with the new school year on 29 August, the 502, 566, 567 and 569 remaining LS-operated with structural alterations, while the 500 passed to Dicksons Travel and new route 666 was added on schooldays. The company took advantage of the large number of ex-West Ham coach-seated LSs that had come out of service, adding LS 35 straight away and phasing more in after repaint. Westlink even managed to get support from Norwich Union to put on a Christmas shoppers' service in Kingston numbered K49 between 30 October and 19 December.

After a long wait, both National Greenways were delivered in October. LS 466 for the Red Arrows was now GLS 1, while high-back-seated GLA 2 (FCA 9X) had most recently been North Western 269 and was new to Crosville. The latter was put into service on the 607 on the 16th, and despite its original mark appreciating in value, 292 CLT had been earmarked for it and was applied in February. GLS 1's renewed service debut was on 4 December on the 505. Meanwhile, there was just one former LBL Leyland National that became a Greenway

under the auspices of London & Country; since it was one of the fleet for contracted route P3 from 2 January 1993 it sneaks into our story. Having been sold in August 1990 and subsequently operated by Blue Triangle, LS 425 came into the hands of the Greenway project in August 1992 and was numbered 342 when it entered service. Commencing a trend to hide the true age of these buses, it was re-registered SIB 6712.

The final event of 1992 for the now severely depleted LS class was the cessation of Harrow Weald's Mobility Bus examples on routes 980-989; these routes passed to London Buslines on 30 November and represented the first withdrawals of Mobility-spec LSs due to London Buslines having their own more modern minibuses to convert. LSs 156 and 308 were stored at Walthamstow, but LS 256 made its way to Capital Citybus, becoming 798 and in effect replacing 795 (LS 356), which, having been out of use since the summer, was progressively dismantled. Meanwhile, Kentish Bus gave their Mobility Bus Nationals local fleetnumbers; LS 202, 290 and LSL 2 becoming 202, 290 and 42.

CHAPTER EIGHT

GREENWAYS AND SONS

Following the receipt of GLS 1 and 2, it was announced that 41 more Leyland Nationals would be receiving the Greenway treatment, and in January 1993 LS 506 was the first to be sent to Reigate garage, where a section was set aside for the conversions. Seven more were despatched there from storage at Fulwell during March, and three more in April. The opportunity was taken starting at this point to re-register examples, depending on what available RM marks could be matched to existing LS fleetnumbers.

Westlink's LS 84, equipped with an experimental exit door-edge sensor and for a very long time the only example to wear the original livery of that concern, was repainted in February 1993. LS 9 had had enough and was taken apart for spares, helping repair LS 153 and accident-damaged LS 96. On 6 March the 468 was extended from Epsom to Epsom

Hospital and on 4 April the portion of the 578 operated was subsumed back into London & Country's 479. Westlink itself was offered for sale on 5 May as the vanguard of privatisation of the rest of the LBL companies.

Walthamstow's post-closure spell as a storage site ended on 30 April, LSs 156 and 308 having been driven to Fulwell eight days earlier. Capital Citybus's normal Mobility Bus LSs were up to some unusual tricks during May, with 796 on the commercial routes 348 and 323 on the 13th, followed by LT route 246, and 797 sneaking out onto LT route 153 during the evening of 4 May! Capital Citybus took several second-hand National 2s that spring and followed up with the purchase of LSs 176 and 288, which were renumbered 736 and 737; although meant for the company's burgeoning Essex commercials they occasionally infiltrated LT work in their four years at Dagenham.

Right: **With Canary Wharf in the background during May 1993, Capital Citybus 798 (THX 256S) shows how wheelchair passengers (and in this case, a shopping trolley) are boarded.** *Haydn Davies*

LS 288 remained to dual-door format, not being single-doored (as B44F) and painted yellow until October; LS 176 had been repainted by Greengates of Plaistow. 794 spent the morning peak of 11 May on the 215 and the evening peak on the 257. London & Country 342 will have undoubtedly been among the Greenways there to wander from the P3 to the 78 and 85 on occasion, the last mentioned on attachment to Addlestone. The Red Arrow network's own

Greenways were now coming back, the pace of conversion picking up by May. Each bus was reclassified GLS to match its new configuration, although GLS 1 was not renumbered. Capacity was now B24D+48, adding two standees by comparison with their previous existence as LSs. GLS 486 retained its full seating as B38D, although whether the Saydair-manufactured buckets fitted to the production GLSs deserved the title is debatable!

Right: **The Greenway process is seen in mid-flow during 1993, with this unidentified example at an early stage of completion. The new front is in position, though the cut-out to accommodate the windscreen panels has yet to be done. Comprehensive re-skinning is also evident throughout. This heavy work was designed to give the buses a full decade's extra work, and that was what they got out of it, in a strategy that proved so cost-effective for East Lancs that it let them survive when bigger firms, including, in the end, the mighty Leyland, went to the wall.** *Ian Jordan*

On 17 July the 511 was withdrawn and the 507 came off during evenings and on Saturdays and Sundays. An extra service on the 507 was mounted during the peaks to cover the closure of the main line between Waterloo East and Charing Cross between 26 July and 13 August, and three LSs (455, 465 and 494) were put into Victoria for it, returning the type there albeit temporarily during this garage's phased closure.

Another renumbering affected Kentish Bus's three surviving Mobility Bus LSs on 1 August, 42 (LSL 2), 202 (LS 202) and 290 (LS 290) becoming 492-494. 28 August saw the 218's evening service (now a separate Surrey

contract from the daytime service with London & Country) transferred from Armchair to Westlink, bringing back LSs but coach-seated ones this time. Surrey school route 661, already run by a Westlink Titan, had an LS-operated duplicate added. Repaints continued, including to LS 431 (formerly blue) and LS 13, which lost its Westlink Diplomat names. The open base at Kingston coal yard was vulnerable to vandalism, and once LSs had to be scrambled to the 131 while the damaged vehicles were repaired.

August saw the end of LS 79 and 435 at Stamford Brook, but they were not sold until the end of the year. On the 20th, LS 190 came to

Right: **Examination of the offside of Greenway GLS 493 (GUW 493W), seen at Victoria on 25 February 1994, reveals the unusual treatment of the windows in that the tops have been squared off but not the bottoms. This conversion was completed in October 1993.** *John Laker*

visit Capital Citybus; now in the ownership of Volvo and re-engined by them, it was evaluated for six days on the 246 (and 348) in a blue livery. 794 visited the 215 again on 20 August and 796 tried out Dagenham's 365 on 20 September. Wanderings continued, adding the 298 on 28 October and the 252 on 6 November.

On the occasion of a model railway exhibition at Fairfield Halls on 23 and 24 October, free bus services were laid on by London General, the Sunday contribution being GLS 501 which shadowed the X30 and 403. LS 156, late of Harrow Weald-based Mobility Bus services, returned there in November under LT ownership to be fitted with smartcard-issuing and validating equipment for a new trial. LS 105 was stood down from North Street in December, and an adventure beckoned whereby it joined LS 397 for a joint London United/Centrewest aid trip to Romania in March 1994.

Despite the cancellation of plans for London deregulation, 1994 would turn out to mark the formal dismemberment of unified 'London Transport' operations; one unit, Centrewest, was preparing for this by gradually introducing local names to each of its garages, though the Uxbridge Buses vinyls selected for that particular one were slow to appear, particularly on the 607's LSs and GLS 2. LS 485 had been sent to help out during November and thus dodged Greenway conversion, which process was almost at an end. Four more (LSs 447, 457, 475 and 488) left Waterloo for Fulwell in February, though their tenure was not quite finished either. Completing the exodus of surplus National 2s, LSs 456 and 462 departed in March.

On 6 January 1994 Westlink's LSs commenced new Surrey school route 663 between Walton-on-Thames and Esher via Hersham. The company was then sold on 20 January to its management, taking with it, amongst a welter of other vehicles, 39 LSs (7, 13, 24, 29, 30, 35, 84, 88, 96-99, 112, 116, 123, 150, 153, 195, 227, 245, 251, 259, 268, 297, 304, 335, 337, 363, 373, 381, 385, 395, 405, 408, 411, 422, 429, 431 and 434), of which twelve were unlicensed and LS 363 a trainer. The rest were scheduled for commercial routes 417 and 468 and Surrey routes 218, 501, 566, 567, 569, 572, 582, 592, 602 and 663; wanderings to LT tenders 110, 131 and 371 were commonplace.

Peckham garage closed on 29 January, but the name and code survived on a smaller premises opened the same day just round the corner from Bull Yard. The Mobility Bus routes 931, 932, 933, 936, 937, 970, 971 and 972 made the move with their LSs, but only until 26 February when they passed to Selkent under tender. As Catford used converted MWs, the Nationals' time here had ended and LSs 139, 293 and 320 went into store at Fulwell. North Street, meanwhile, retired LS 105 in December but acquired ex-Harrow Weald LS 308 in February to replace it.

If the ethos of privatisation was strictly about making money, the flipping of Westlink within twelve weeks of its sale fit the description perfectly; on 11 April it was sold on to West Midlands Travel.

During April, three of Uxbridge's LSs (444, 470 and 497) were fitted with Volvo engines. The last two Greenways for Waterloo emerged in May, but the ones that had gone in with full seating kept them, albeit now Saydairs rather than traditional benches; GLSs 448 and 487 seated B38D+23 and GLS 483 B46D+23. The spare LSs found themselves plucked out of store to assist on Wimbledon tennis work, four going into Stockwell and two to Merton. This year's champions were Pete Sampras and Conchita Martinez.

It was now time for Capital Citybus's ex-LSs to leave Mobility Bus work, as on 18 June their Northumberland Park-based 900, 901, 903 (this route renumbered from 973 on 29 January), 906, 907, 908, 909, 910, 920, 921, 922, 923, 924, 925, 927, 929, 947, 948 and 966 were lost on tender to County Bus & Coach. 795 (LS 356) was broken up, while LSs 256 and 396 (ex-798 and 796) came back and were stored at Fulwell, but 794 (LS 454) and 797 (LSL 1) were taken into stock by Capital Citybus, eking out a new role as drivers' restrooms at Chingford Mount with rail replacement work. The normal service examples 736 and 737 soldiered on, during May, June and July ticking off Northumberland Park route 212 and Dagenham's 123, 165 and 345! Between May and 31 August LS 320, having left Peckham, came to help out at Kentish Bus, and on 11 July their routes too were altered, a new 914 coming on and the days of operation of some of the others being shuffled, as was normal for these networks. Peckham's LS 139 was withdrawn in December.

West Midlands Travel-owned Westlink loaned LS 13 to Blue Lake Buses of Chichester from 28 May to mid-June. In August the National 2 came back to Holloway, this time in the form of LSs 464, 465 and 488 as school buses and/or permanent driver trainers.

Privatisation now commenced; on 2 September Centrewest was the first to jump ship, passing to its management. The 607's ten LSs and GLS 2 lost their roundels with the rest of the fleet, but their branding already superseded the future application of local identities so was left alone. Only LS 484 and 495 had Uxbridge Buses fleetnames. On the 6th Stagecoach bought East London and Selkent, the only Nationals in the combined fleet comprising North Street-based Mobility Bus LSs 121, 308 and 403 leased from LT, and LS 403 spread its wings in the second half of October via one visit to the 247 and twice on the 499. The three LSs recently into Holloway left LBL with the rest of London Northern on 26 October, by which time they had been joined by LS 489. MTL Trust Holdings was the new owner.

Westlink sent six of its spare LSs (84, 153, 268, 373, 405 and 429) up to its West Midlands Travel parent early in September to assume former Stevensons routes in Uttoxeter and Burton, while in town their evening participation on the 218 was given up to London Buslines on 3

Below: **The rear aspect of the National Greenway was neat and tidy, though the rear blind box (an indulgence continued only by London operators, since it was a contractual requirement) has migrated below the rear window to enable its access by pulling aside the rear seat bench. Seen crossing Lambeth Bridge in September 1994, GLS 502 (GUW 502W) is symbolically saying goodbye to London Transport, all its roundels bar the one within the rear logo having been removed. It is also actually on route 507.** *Haydn Davies*

THE LONDON LS

September. Another loan was made to Blue Lake, in the form of LS 434 this time, and in November LS 13 headed that way too. Uxbridge's LSs and GLS 2 added Buckinghamshire County Council route 335 to their portfolio on 5 September (invariably using LS 484, one of the non-branded ones), but lost the similar U1 augmentation on 1 October when much of that route's outer portion was devolved to Hertfordshire County Council as MA-operated R1. All the LSs had been fitted with Volvo engines by this point, and additionally LS 475 had its rear blind box panelled over and had to carry a sticker for the route number.

When London General was sold to its management on 2 November it inherited 42 GLSs and three unaltered LSs, but these three were taken out of Waterloo in November and sent to Sutton for use on the Epsom Park and Ride commencing on the 19th. That was all the LS operators now in the private sector, although fleets were in motion already as MTL London Northern could identify no further use for its

four LSs and moved them on to its parent in Liverpool in January 1995.

In October Capital Citybus 794 (LS 454) was upseated from B24DL to B41F, renumbered 744 and repainted yellow, passing from Northumberland Park to Dagenham for normal service; two new commercial services had been activated there that required single-deckers. The sizeable fleet of Nationals over and above the ex-LT examples were also used on the 252 on Sundays during November due to a diversion.

Westlink's 131 was split across Kingston on 29 October and a new route 411 created to cover the West Molesey end; although Titan-operated and later given over to three Metrobuses sourced from the parent WMT, it soon saw LSs. LS 245 was repainted in October into a new livery of red with a much broader white band with a turquoise one within; LS 411 followed suit in November, but subsequent repaints were to the existing style. Repaints to the 371's DWLs meant LSs turning out on the 371 much more than of late.

British Bus plc now had Kentish Bus and London & Country within the same portfolio, and on 1 January 1995 consolidated the LT tendered operations of each into a new organisation called Londonlinks; the P3 and its Walworth-based Greenways (plus 342 in our account) were included. London General's three original LSs at Sutton worked on not only the Tesco free bus to New Malden but the 393, normally the province of DWs.

Despite all the upheaval of the last year, the LS and Greenway operations split over five companies settled down as their new identities consolidated. Tendering kept the four Red Arrow routes with London General with the existing GLSs, which were fitted with Wayfarer ticket machines to go with their fareboxes in time for the 19 June start); the ticket issuing unit was actually on the bulkhead behind the cab. An MM-sized box for a side blind was also fitted in the first window, and fluorescent blind sets were printed for the entire operation of four routes. The three surviving LSs worked the Chelsea Flower Show on 25 May, all by now having not only new London General fleetnames (so far quite rare) but 'LG' garage codes.

At Capital Citybus, just about anything could appear on anything. 797 (ex-LSL 1) was duly repainted yellow and put back into service in March, by which time the yellow ex-LSs had chalked up the 296 on their visits. On 15 April four (including 744) were transferred from Dagenham to Northumberland Park for the Easter weekend so that an equivalent number of minibuses could be put to work on rail replacement. That ensured 'LS' visits to the 298.

On 6 May Westlink's 216 had augmentations that resulted in the withdrawal of the 572 and 582; the 436's early-morning Westlink journeys came off at the same time. The company then won the 81 on 29 July, setting it going with the Deltas from the 110, which was replenished with the 371's DWLs, plus LSs on its first two days until the 371's new Optare Vectas were put into service on 1 August, when their 'N' registrations became legal. Naturally, LSs soon visited the new acquisition. Dayglo blinds began to make their appearance from April, as they were doing across all contracted fleets, and LS 422 was fitted with a video screen behind the driver (British Bus companies' on-board entertainment).

Stagecoach East London's three Mobility Buses, LSs 121, 308 and 403, moved to Barking in April but returned in June, even though LS 403 was turned out on the 499 on 3 May. These routes (935 and 949-962 inclusive, with alterations) departed the arena through their takeup by Thamesway on 28 October, leaving just the Kentish Bus set, which had themselves been tendered but retained. The three ex-North Street LSs were sold to Ensign in November.

Westlink repainted LS 112 into a white-based advert livery with blue lettering, extolling Epsom-area Volkswagen dealer John Ashley and accordingly was rostered on local route 468. The company's summer and autumn were otherwise as follows; on 8 July its 417 was extended from Egham to Windsor Castle, and on the 29th the 216 was transferred on Sunday from Kingston to Hounslow Heath, restoring LSs on that day of the week (although on 20 August enough DWLs were made spare from

the 110 to return). On 2 September the 602 was extended to Hounslow and the the 402 was taken on from London & Country. Their use on former Stevensons routes having come to an end comparatively quickly, the six LSs seconded to the parent were returned between September and year's end. But the major happening for Westlink in 1995 was the company's takeover by London United on 15 September. The 411 was thus transferred to the new parent on the 23rd, a week earlier than planned, and to fill the gap at Kingston the 216 was transferred back from Hounslow Heath. On the 30th the 567 was transferred to Javelin other than on Saturdays, and school route 663 passed to London & Country.

33 LSs came with the transfer (LSs 7, 13, 24, 29, 30, 35, 88, 96-99, 112, 116, 123, 150, 195, 227, 245, 251, 259, 297, 304, 335, 337, 363, 381, 385, 395, 408, 411, 422, 431 and 434) and of these LS 227, fitted with a wheelchair lift in its exit doorway, was given an all-over livery in white (plus a blue flash) for Kingston University. LS 373, on attachment to West Midlands Travel, was fitted with a DAF engine and LSs 123 and 245 were converted to single-door (with a capacity of DP40F). In November LS 381 was seconded to Shepherd's Bush as a trainer and on the 18th of that month economies were made by transferring the 81 to Hounslow on Sundays so that Hounslow Heath could close on that day of the week.

Centrewest finished 1995 with the re-registration of GLS 2 from 292 CLT to WPC 316X so that the Routemaster mark could go onto LX 2; having strayed off the 607 just once in its spell at Uxbridge (to the 222), the Greenway was sold on 15 November. The coach-seated LSs, of which LS 495 was now in the 607's livery, continued to wander to the 222 and U1, though the U1's official LS augmentation finished on 1 October, and on 16 December LS 503 visited the U4 carrying slipboards in lieu of blinds. London General's three Sutton-based LSs were put to work on the Kingston-New Malden section of the 213 to offset traffic problems caused by roadworks in Tolworth. GLS 448 was reported to have turned out on the 211 during the evening peak of 22 November. GLS 479 was repainted allover red in August and in December received a new Red Arrow logo designed by Best Impressions, but as it turned out, this would remain unique. A yellow band did appear at the top of the grey band upon repaint, GLS 460 being the first in the spring of 1996.

There had been National Greenways, but a revised and simplified programme undertaken later was waggishly christened 'Son of Greenway' before a more official, and much blander name of 'Urban Bus' was adopted for such conversions. At the close of 1995 eight of Westlink's spare LSs (84, 153, 268, 297, 335, 373, 395 and 405) were earmarked for this work, which would retain their external appearance other than taking out the centre door.

Capital Citybus was sold to its management on 21 December after five years with the CNT Group, obliging, after a while, new logos. Appearances of its former LSs on LT tenders during 1995 and into 1996 had added the 165, 248, 252, 365 and D6, usually when rail replacement work employed those routes' normal vehicles. 797 was out of action after an accident in April and had gone by October.

On 10 February 1996 Westlink diverted some of its route 468 journeys to Mansfield Park rather than Chessington World of Adventures.

In February the only other Greenway to qualify for this account, Londonlinks 342, was repainted into that undertaking's new livery. Its regular berth on the P3 was shared with Titans, Volvo Citybuses and a bit of everything else available at Walworth.

The separated paths of two strains of ex-London Transport LSs unexpectedly crossed when on 4 April London General loaned LSs 445 and 453 to Westlink, which put them out on the 216 on the 4th, 6th and 9th of that month. The refurbished LSs were now earmarked for the H37 at Hounslow, representing a move from Westlink to London United. Despite the replacement of their heating, the nine examples retained their roof pods, though the single doors were now two-leaf variants and the whole powered by a Volvo engine with a new gearbox; no reclassification was undertaken. Neither Son of Greenway nor Urban Bus as such, the refurbishments bought these now almost twenty-year-old buses a new lease of life. Now to B38F capacity with new flooring and seating, LS 153 was first out of the Crawley works of London & Country where this work was now done, being towed into Hounslow on 26 March.

Left: **Late in the day for the LS, there were still surprises to be found, and none more than when London General's unaltered National 2s went a-wandering. LS 445 (GUW 445W) and 453 were loaned to neighbouring London United and turned out on the 216 on three days in April 1996.**
Haydn Davies

The official conversion date of the H37, which also added the LXs to make up the numbers, was 29 June, but LS 153 entered service on 4 April and the rest started trickling in dribs and drabs between April and November. With five more added to the original complement during the process, the full set of thirteen comprised LSs 84, 96, 99, 153, 268, 298, 335, 337, 373, 385, 395, 405 and 431. They looked splendid in London United's post-privatisation livery of red with two shades of grey, but then again, what didn't? Naturally, the flexibility inherent at Hounslow led the new/old acquisitions to wander, LS 153 trying out the commercial 555/556 pair and another on the 120 during May, followed by the H22 in June. As early as July they had ticked off the 81, 111, H32, H91 and H98 as well and such would be the case for the four more years they were in service. The 116 was taken up by London United on 31 August, and the LXs still in Hounslow would be joined on it by LSs from the outset, and new route 235, instituted on the same date, also quickly added LSs to its scheduled Ms.

Below: **No livery flattered modern bus lines like that of London United, and the Urban Bus conversions put into action on the H37 in 1996 belied their otherwise high calendar age. LS 99 (OJD 899R) in August 1998 shows the full treatment, with two-leaf doors, DiPTAC green handrails (which otherwise hadn't reached the LS class as a whole) and new Volvo engines. The roof pods stayed put despite changes to the ventilation system; they weren't doing any harm where they were.**
Haydn Davies

Capital Citybus's 'LSs' spent their 1996 popping up on new conquests for them in the shape of school routes 645 and 652 (the latter until its loss on 28 September), while new route 511 introduced on 21 February also became fair game before long. They also helped out on a service intended to cover for the DLR during May while its infrastructure was rebuilt following terrorist bombing. However, the two LT routes best suited to these single-deckers, the 246 and 446, were withdrawn on 27 September. The buses' main work remained the ever-changing spread of commercials out to Lakeside, which by the autumn of 1996 were known as 323, 324 and 349.

Westlink added an 833 over part of the K3 (which continued to see regular LSs) on 28 June and the next day Hounslow Heath took over the H23 from London United's Hounslow, quickly putting out its LSs where the regular DRs failed. On 31 August its LSs started a new Surrey route 416 that filled in for the 116's lost section between Ashford and Staines; Hounslow joined in during the peaks. Underscoring its new status as part of London United, the Hounslow Heath depot took the H91 and the bulk of the H22 (from Hounslow) when Stamford Brook was mothballed, and LS appearances were a foregone conclusion.

Other than the core of GLSs at London General (bought by the Go-Ahead Group on 23 May and its buses soon having their stickers added), the refurbished LSs at London United and the mavericks at Capital Citybus, two other National operations came to a close in 1996. First finished the adventures of Londonlinks 342 and its partners, which were eased off the P3 during August and September when transfers of Volvo Citybuses allowed it to be converted to double-deck operation. In any case, the route was lost to Stagecoach Selkent on 2 November and 342 was moved out to Maidstone & District. Then, the enormously popular 607 route at Centrewest was retendered and retained, but promoted to double-deck with new Volvo Olympians, which replaced them between 27 September and 12 October. The length of the LSs made them perfect candidates for training buses, given that the mandatory length for such buses was increasing, and over the next few months six of the ten were fitted out as such and repainted into the attractive yellow and red livery Centrewest used for its trainers. Now that Centrewest had purchased Bee Line, the LS trainers were often seen at the latter's Southall premises, though the general base for such work was Acton Tram Depot.

London General also sold LSs 445, 448 and 482 in November 1996; one of their uses this year had been on the Hampton Court Flower Show service in July, but an attempt to find permanent work for them on a Surrey route was foiled when London & Country took it up instead. The Red Arrow routes soldiered on quietly with their GLSs, which during 1997 gradually began to receive the yellow bands separating the red and grey of the company's established livery.

Westlink had been phasing in a new livery of red with a diagonal grey front and a new logo, but the only LS to receive it was LS 7 (ex-East London red and gold) at the end of 1996, after a prolonged period out of use; its usual spot was on the 468, which had been revised on 30 November to lose its Mansfield Park leg and operate at all times to Chessington. A plan to close Kingston garage and reallocate its services (including LS-operated 216, 468 and 833) to a new site in Hampton Wick on 28 June fell through and the garage remained open on an extended lease. That date nonetheless saw the 592 withdrawn. A further attempt to get shot of Kingston by moving the 216, 468 and K3 into Fulwell on 30 August also came to naught, but an overspill site at Kingsgate Road was taken on a temporary basis. Even so, the LS era was drawing slowly to an end, with DRs increasingly preferred on the 417, 566 and 569.

Below: **Another stab at a new livery by Westlink treated LS 7 (KJD 507P) to this likeable scheme of red with a grey front, exploring a theme Best Impressions had become fond of and which would later reach its apex with Arriva. Like that of LS 245, this livery didn't settle either and, other than gracing a Metrorider, was not repeated, and in fact Westlink's identity was to be subsumed into London United thereafter, livery and all. The bus is seen in July 1997.** *Haydn Davies*

Three surplus LSs (8, 408 and 434) had been sent to Stamford Brook for store in June and LSs 29 and 116 were cannibalised for parts. Finally, sales began, LSs 97, 98, 116, 408 and 434 going in December and LSs 13, 30, 97 and 304 in February 1998 (though in LS 30's case only as far as Metro Travel in Hounslow). Retaining its Westlink livery, LS 13 became the first 'LT' LS in preservation, nearly 25 years after the class had entered service.

On 19 June Capital Citybus sold 736 (LS 176) and 737 (LS 288) to Dart of Paisley. The only ex-LT LS left here was now 744, but it would stay put for nearly three more years. Kentish Bus, meanwhile, spent a calm 1997, losing just the 928 to Javelin on 4 August, but in the autumn the company became part of the wholesale rebranding of British Bus's operations to Arriva. Although remaining in red where everything else had to assume the new turquoise livery, the three Mobility Bus Nationals underwent a further renumbering on 30 November, adding three thousand to their fleetnumbers to render them 3492-3494.

On 10 January 1998 the 216 was reallocated from Kingston to Hounslow Heath, taking with it LSs 88, 112, 123, 259, 411 and 422, and the 417 was withdrawn altogether. Only LSs 7, 195 and 227 were now allocated to Kingston. Hounslow's LSs lost the chance to appear on the 235 with its move to Tellings-Golden Miller but gained one with the move in of the 110 from Hounslow Heath. The conversion of the 116 from LX to M made no difference to the ability of LSs to appear on it, nor on any other

Hounslow route operated at the time, barring the 140. Westlink was winding down both in terms of LSs operated and company identity, as by 1998 all new acquisitions and existing minibuses were labelled with London United logos. The last permanently LS-operated LT route at Hounslow Heath was the 216, which from 29 August was restocked with DWLs repainted into London United red and greys.

The rest of the LSs were withdrawn during the summer and into the autumn, the last two (LS 411 and 429) surviving until November. DAF-engined LSs 195 and 227 (unofficially reclassified 'DLS') were deemed worth keeping, however, and in October were repainted from Kingston University white into London United red and greys to keep the National presence alive on the 566 and 567 out of Hounslow Heath (now officially coded HH and with those codes displayed on bus sides). These two could still drift to LT routes, LS 227 making a visit to the H22 on 25 March plus a first time on the R70's school bus duty WK995 (or HH995) and LS 195 revisiting the 81 twice. The announcement in September of the H37's retention by London United with new Dart SLFs in 1999 set the clock ticking on the modernised LSs' own tenure.

On 2 April 1998 Kentish Bus was renamed Arriva Kent Thameside and on 8 July Capital Citybus became First Capital upon its purchase by FirstGroup. Centrewest sold two of its training LSs during 1998, three more in 1999 (including LS 503, which gave up its 503 CLT plate in April in preparation) and the last one of all, LS 504, lingered until September 2000. As

Left: **On 28 April 1999, as forms were being signed that would replace the H37's stalwart LSs with new Dennis Dart SLFs, Hounslow had stuck LS 153 (THX 153S) out on the 111 as AV55, and in mid-afternoon it is seen backing out of stop A7 at Kingston bus station.** *Author*

the millennium came upon us, it was now time to take off the stragglers finally; First Capital 744 (LS 454) finally finished in June 2000, having spent much of its time on the Excel-intended 396 with its non-LT-derived partners (and even, on 26 June 1999, the 1!), and the three LSs (3492-3494, a.k.a LSL 2, LS 202 and LS 290) on Arriva Kent Thameside's stalwart Mobility Bus routes (911-919 and 930) anchored on Croydon came off at last after service on 31 March when their routes were lost to Crystals for takeup after the Easter weekend. Their kingdom had never been threatened other than by one low-floor Scania once in 1998, but now all new buses were low-floor and the Mobility Bus routes themselves could begin to wither away, their job done. 3494 marked the occasion with reference on its rear window to it having spent ten years on Croydon Mobility Bus services, and in this respect it was the last Mark I LS on any type of London stage service.

At London United, the H37's Dart SLFs were included in an order for 82 placed in April 1999, and the batch intended for this route entered service at Hounslow late in July, after which the 'Urban Bus' LSs were withdrawn. Just LSs 195 and 227 remained at London United now, carrying on on the 566 and 567 until they too were withdrawn after 2 August, putting to an end an odyssey that had spanned almost a quarter of a century unbroken. LS 195 was out that day on the 81. Even after all the LSs (refurbished and not) had been sold, LSs 153, 297, 405 and 431 were kept on as trainers, prolonging their lives into the new millennium, and three of them made a further move to another company subsequently acquired,

Sovereign. This undertaking had formerly included BTS and retained their half of Edgware garage, where LSs 153, 297 and 431 were put to work, the latter two racking up over a year each. Sold in December 2004, LSs 297 and 431 were the very last LSs in the ownership of any post-LBL company.

That wasn't even the end in London for the ex-London LSs, as Thorpes bought LSs 84, 96, 99, 195, 227, 268, 335, 337 and 395 of them to furnish a nine-bus PVR of a Jubilee Line standby contract applying from 1 January

Below: **The Millennium Dome may have been mildly embarrassing as an event, but nobody could say it wasn't ready, and nor were the standby buses mounted in considerable numbers just in case. Although LS 335 (AYR 335T) is actually away from its base when caught in Stratford on 12 August 2000, it's empty; the Jubilee Line was reliable enough.** *Author*

Right: **London General took the tapegrey livery it inherited from LBL and added a yellow band. A couple of years further on, it turned the grey skirt to a dark shade of charcoal. All this didn't help the 505, however, which made way for an extension of the 243 along its entirety to Waterloo. On 18 August 2000, the 505's last day, GLS 486 (186 CLT, ex-GUW 486W) stands at Shoreditch.** *Author*

to 31 December 2000; the other seven were allocated to Blue Triangle. The Jubilee Line extension would prove reliable enough that the buses sat about idle most of the time, in spite of being joined by two Metrobuses, and it was terminated early, on 13 October.

In stage service terms, all that remained by 2000 was the Red Arrow fleet, which was protected on its limited routes enough to suffer almost no mishaps, but the GLSs' lives were far from dull. GLS 478 once turned out with a conductor on the 11 on 25 November 1998 when an RML couldn't be mustered. A very

late re-registration was of GLS 463 to WLT 463 in February 1999 after M 463, that mark's previous host, was sold, and in May GLS 1 was renumbered GLS 466. The new skirt colour of charcoal grey spread to the GLS fleet at the turn of the century, beginning in July 2000 with GLS 486 and having spread to most of them through overall repaint by the following spring. However, their route roster dwindled; from 19 August 2000 (to accompany the extension by fifteen months of the existing London General contracts, after which the effects of the Jubilee Line extension would be taken into account

Right and inset: **The new Red Arrow logo premiered on GLS 479 (GUW 479W) promised great things, based as it was on the existing London General post-privatisation theme, but, like a lot of ideas of the time, never got beyond the prototype. On 18 August 2000 the combination is seen at London Bridge.** *Author*

by the planners), the 505 was withdrawn and appended to the 243 and the 501 was folded into the 521. While the overall PVR dropped by four, GLSs 487 and 496, two of the fully-seated variety, were put to work on the hospital contract service taken over from Putney Darts. GLS 483 was loaned to Metrobus and amazingly, on 4 October 2001 crept out on the 146 as GD25! Finally, the 507 and 521 were tendered again in July 2001 and the award was made contingent upon London General ordering 31 bendy buses; Mercedes-Benz Citaro Gs. Three GLSs were sold in October 2001 and a fourth (accident-damaged GLS 501) in March, leaving 38 in service at Waterloo. The last day of the GLS, and thus any National in London service, was 31 May 2002, with GLS 477 on the 507 ushering the class out. Like the London United LSs before them, rail replacement standby work was their immediate employment post-withdrawal, twenty of the GLSs going to a joint venture formed for this purpose by Blue Triangle and Mike Nash straight after coming off service. London General kept the remaining eighteen around with the same idea, though they were all sold by the end of 2002.

CHAPTER NINE

AFTER SERVICE

More LSs than you'd think survive in preservation, coming later to it after the Leyland National's unintended but remarkable longevity enabled plenty to continue in service with subsequent operators well into the 21st century, with or without a re-engining and/or conversion to single-door. The most cherished of these, the Walsall-based network of Chase Coaches, fielded a large fleet of predominantly LT-derived LSs until 28 April 2007, with ex-London Country SNBs also featuring. Some of those have appeared on the rally circuit, although LS 193 is now wearing a Bexleybus livery it never actually carried. LS 35 keeps the East London red and gold alive and LS 7 exemplifies the Westlink days, while LSs 24, 98 and 103 recall when they were new to London Transport. LS 13, on the other hand, took its Westlink livery to Australia and continues to wear it in Sydney. Fewer National 2s and their Greenway descendants survive, but LS 444 is the best known of the former and GLS 443 represents the latter.

Below: **A decade and a half after Mark I Nationals had left squadron service in London, Chase Coaches in Walsall had collected not only two dozen former LSs, but examples of London Country SNBs and B-series Nationals new to Ribble. On 28 April 2007, the company's gala last day before absorption into one of the local Arriva chapters, ex-LS 193 (THX 193S) still with dual doors passes ex-LS 209 (THX 209S) underneath the 'landed flying saucer' canopy of Walsall bus station. The second LS mentioned was one of three Chase buses to go into Arriva livery to prepare passengers for the takeover.** *Author*

Left: **On 19 July 2015 preserved LS 24 (KJD 524P) is performing shuttle runs to and from the Alton bus rally at Anstey Park.** *Author*

Left: **North Weald bus rally was held for the last time on 21 June 2015, and one of its entrants was LS 35 (KJD 535P), immortalised in the elegant gold-accented livery used by LBL's East London subsidiary for West Ham-based LS operations.** *Author*

Left: **The future of bus rallies lies in running days operated on a fares-free basis, thus not disrupting regular stage services and encouraging voluntary contributions. Slough's regular event saw LS 444 (GUW 444W) operating on 1 June 2014.** *Author*

APPENDICES

Registrations

LS 1-6	TGY 101-106M
LS 7-57	KJD 507-557P
LS 58-107	OJD 858-907R
LS 108-267	THX 108-267S
LS 268-297	YYE 268-297T
LS 298-355	AYR 298-355T
LS 356-437	BYW 356-437V
LS 438-506	GUW 438-506W

Leyland codes

LS 1-6	1051/2R
LS 7-437	10351A/2R
LS 438-506	NL106AL11/2R

London Transport codes

LS 1-6	1LS1
LS 7-437	2LS2
LS 438-506	3LS3
Upseated P4 examples 3LS3/1	

Re-registrations

LS 443	WLT 843 (04.93)
LS 448	WLT 648 (04.93)
LS 463	WLT 463 (02.99)
LS 467	WLT 467 (06.93)
LS 480	VLT 180 (04.93)
LS 483	83 CLT (06.93)
GLS 486	186 CLT (07.93)
LS 487	WLT 487 (04.93)
LS 496	WLT 696 (05.93)
GLS 498	WLT 598 (02.94)
GLS 499	WLT 599 (01.94)
	GUW 499W (12.98)
LS 503	503 CLT (01.92)
	GUW 503W (03.99)
GLS 2	292 CLT (02.93)
	WPC 316X (11.95)

Right: August 1987 sees Bromley's LS 95 (OJD 895R) on the 227 with the Crystal Palace transmission mast as a backdrop . *Haydn Davies*

Chassis Numbers

LS 1-6	00703, 00775, 00776, 00817-00819
LS 7-57	03485-03494, 03552-03561, 03586-03595, 03601-03610, 03620-03630
LS 58-107	04283-04286, 04306-04309, 04327-04330, 04348-04351, 04368-04371, 04387-04390, 04406-04409, 04423-04426, 04445-04448, 04454-04457, 04474-04477, 04496-04499, 04507, 04508
LS 108-267	04808-04817, 04819, 04820, 04823, 04824, 04834, 04840, 04841, 04847-04851, 04854, 04863-04865, 04873-04875, 04878, 04879, 04883, 04884, 04889, 04890, 04893, 04898-04900, 04903, 04904, 04907, 04908, 04913, 04914, 04916, 04917, 04920-04922, 04926, 04927, 04929, 04930, 04932, 04935, 04936, 04939, 04940, 04943, 04946, 04947, 04950, 04951, 04955, 04969, 04970, 04973, 04976, 04977, 04991, 04992, 05000, 05001, 05006, 05007, 05010, 05011, 05019, 05020, 05026, 05027, 05031, 05037, 05038, 05042, 05043, 05054, 05057, 05058, 05076, 05077, 05109-05111, 05132, 05133, 05134, 05139, 05140, 05144, 05145, 05151-05153, 05159-05161, 05162, 05166-05168, 05173-05176, 05180-05182, 05189-05191, 05194, 05195, 05203, 05204, 05207-05210, 05239-05241, 05246, 05247, 05259, 05260, 05264, 05271, 05272, 05277, 05278, 05281-05283, 05298-05300, 05310, 05311, 05331, 05332, 05335-05337, 05342, 05343, 05349-05351
LS 268-297	05762, 05766, 05770, 05776, 05777, 05780, 05781, 05784, 05785, 05788, 05789, 05796, 05797, 05800, 05801, 05804, 05805, 05808, 05809, 05812, 05813, 05818, 05819, 05822, 05823, 05864, 05865, 05868, 05881, 05882
LS 298-437	06116, 06119, 06121, 06123, 06125, 06154, 06156, 06158, 06178, 06180, 06183, 06185, 06187, 06190, 06192, 06210, 06212, 06214, 06216, 06218, 06228, 06230, 06232, 06234, 06236, 06244, 06246, 06248, 06250, 06252, 06262, 06264, 06267, 06272, 06274, 06285, 06287, 06289, 06294, 06296, 06300, 06302, 06305, 06307, 06311, 06313, 06316, 06317, 06324, 06325, 06327, 06329, 06333, 06334, 06339, 06340, 06346, 06347, 06350, 06351,06356, 06357, 06360, 06361, 06364, 06365, 06370, 06371, 06377, 06382, 06383, 06386, 06387, 06392, 06393, 06397, 06402, 06403, 06406, 06407, 06412, 06413, 06418, 06419, 06424, 06425, 06428, 06429, 06435, 06436, 06439, 06440, 06449, 06450, 06453, 06454, 06457, 06458, 06465, 06466, 06469, 06470, 06475, 06476, 06482, 06483, 06489, 06490, 06493, 06494, 06497, 06498, 06501, 06502, 06506, 06507, 06514, 06515, 06518, 06519, 06522, 06523, 06531, 06532, 06535, 06536, 06539, 06540, 06543, 06544, 06549, 06550, 06555, 06556, 06561, 06562, 06567, 06568, 06571, 06572
LS 438-506	07162, 07321-07329, 07331-07342, 07346-07375, 07394-07402, 07427-07434

Renumberings

LS 466 to GLS 1, 10.92
GLS 1 to GLS 466, 05.99

Bexleybus Fleetnumbers

41	LS 18	**47**	LS 82	**53**	LS 178	**59**	LS 294
42	LS 21	**48**	LS 120	**54**	LS 184	**60**	LS 315
43	LS 28	**49**	LS 126	**55**	LS 186	**61**	LS 316
44	LS 31	**50**	LS 135	**56**	LS 239	**62**	LS 328
45	LS 50	**51**	LS 137	**57**	LS 282	**63**	LS 389
46	LS 73	**52**	LS 155	**58**	LS 284	**64***	LS 428

* LS 428 renumbered from 64 to 58, 02.89

Acquired second-hand

05.82   1234L (SCO 422L), 11.3/B46D, new to Plymouth City Transport 1972 (22).
          Sold 06.89
10.90   LSL 1 (WYJ 165S), 11.3/B25DL+7, new to Southdown 1977 (65).
          To Capital Citybus 11.91
06.91   LSL 2 (RUF 42R), 11.3/B44D, new to Southdown 1977 (42).
          To Kentish Bus 07.91
10.92   GLS 2 (FCA 9X), DP49F+21, ex-North Western (269), new to Crosville 1982 (SNL 9)
          Converted to Greenway by 10.92. Sold 11.95

Converted to Greenway specification (and reclassified GLS)

LSs 438-440, 442, 443, 446, 448-450, 452, 455, 459, 460, 463, 466*, 467-469, 471, 473, 474, 476-481, 483, 486, 487, 490-493, 496, 498-502, 505, 506
* Prototype; reclassified GLS 1

Date of Greenway conversion

10.92	GLS 1	12.93	GLS 440, 467, 479, 492
05.93	GLS 468, 491, 506	01.94	GLS 455, 460
06.93	GLS 439, 449, 469, 471, 474, 481, 486, 501	02.94	GLS 438, 446, 477, 500
07.93	GLS 442, 476	03.94	GLS 473, 480, 487
09.93	GLS 450, 478, 490	04.94	GLS 443, 452
10.93	GLS 493, 496, 498, 499, 502, 505	05.94	GLS 448, 483
11.93	GLS 459, 463		

Delivered

07.73	LS 1
08.73	LS 2
09.73	LS 4, 6
10.73	LS 3, 5
05.76	LS 7-9, 11-15
06.76	LS 16, 19-21, 23, 30
07.76	LS 10, 17, 18, 22, 24-29, 31-35, 37-43
08.76	LS 36, 44-50
09.76	LS 51-57
03.77	LS 58, 59, 62-66, 68
04.77	LS 60, 61, 67, 69-85
05.77	LS 86-98, 101
06.77	LS 99, 100, 102-107
11.77	LS 108-117, 119-122, 125-127, 129
12.77	LS 118, 123, 128, 131-141, 147, 148, 151-153, 156
01.78	LS 124, 130, 142-145, 149, 154, 155, 157-159, 162-164, 166-168, 170-174
02.78	LS 146, 150, 160, 161, 169, 175, 176, 184
03.78	LS 165, 177, 179, 182, 183, 185, 186, 188, 189, 191-193, 195, 197, 198, 201, 203, 204
04.78	LS 178, 180, 199, 202, 205-208, 210, 211, 217, 218, 220, 223
05.78	LS 190, 200, 209, 212-214, 219, 221, 224-237, 239, 241, 242
06.78	LS 194, 238, 240, 243-249, 252-263
07.78	LS 181, 196, 264, 266, 267
08.78	LS 250, 251, 265
09.78	LS 187, 216, 222
10.78	LS 215
12.78	LS 268-278, 282, 283, 285
01.79	LS 279-281, 284, 286-292, 295
02.79	LS 293, 294, 296, 297
05.79	LS 298-305, 310, 311
06.79	LS 306-309, 312-317, 319
07.79	LS 318, 320-323, 325-330, 332-337
08.79	LS 331, 338-341, 343-347, 349, 351, 352, 354, 356-358, 361, 365, 369
09.79	LS 342, 348, 350, 353, 355, 359, 362-364, 366-368, 370-373, 375, 378-381, 384-386
10.79	LS 324, 360, 374, 376, 377, 382, 383, 388-397, 300-405, 407, 414
11.79	LS 387, 398, 399, 406, 408-412, 415, 419-421, 424, 427-437
12.79	LS 416-418, 422, 423
01.80	LS 413, 426
02.81	LS 438-455, 458, 459, 461, 462, 465-467, 472-474, 476, 479-482, 486, 488
03.81	LS 456, 457, 460, 463, 464, 489
04.81	LS 470, 490-492
05.81	LS 468, 469, 471, 475, 478, 483-485, 487, 493, 495-506
06.81	LS 494
07.81	LS 477

Into Service

11.73	LS 1-6 (**D**)
08.76	LS 8-11, 16-40, 42, 43, 45 (**AV**)
09.76	LS 7, 14, 41, 44, 46-49, 51-56 (**AV**)
10.76	LS 12, 13, 15, 50, 57 (**AV**)
06.77	LS 60-64, 66-68, 70-84, 87 (**ED**), LS 85 (**AV**)
07.77	LS 65, 89 (**AV**), LS 88 (**ED**)
08.77	LS 58, 59, 69, 82, 90-101, 103-105, 107 (**TB**)
01.78	LS 102, 106 (**AV**)
02.78	LS 86, 115-119, 121-134 (**RD**), LS 108-114 (**W**)
03.78	LS 120 (**RD**)
04.78	LS 135-141, 148, 150 (**FW**), LS 142-147, 149, 151, 152, 154, 155, 157, 160, 195 (**PR**)
05.78	LS 153, 156, 158, 159, 162, 164, 167, 169, 173 (**T**), LS 161, 163, 171, 188, 192, 197, 198, 201, 203, 204, 218 (**D**)
06.78	LS 165, 176, 177, 191 (**D**), LS 166, 170, 178, 189, 193, 199, 201, 203, 204, 231 (**MH**), LS 172, 174, 185, 186 (**HT**), LS 179 (**T**), LS 212 (**FW**)
07.78	LS 180, 182-184, 190, 194, 200, 202 (**L**)

09.78	LS 205, 207, 209, 210, 213, 214, 217, 219-221, 223, 224 (**HL**)
	LS 225-229, 232, 235, 236, 238, 239, 243, 247 (**V**)
10.78	LS 237, 240, 241, 244-246, 248, 249 (**HD**)
	LS 250, 251, 253-255, 259, 260, 262, 263 (**PM**)
11.78	LS 187, 196, 216, 222, 223, 257, 258, 266 (**ED**), LS 211, 234, 242, 252, 261, 264, 265 (**PM**)
12.78	LS 256 (**AV**), LS 267 (**ED**)
03.79	LS 181, 206, 268, 272, 273, 278, 279, 284, 289, 292, 294 (**NB**),
	LS 270, 271, 274, 275, 277, 281, 283, 285-287, 295, 297 (**T**)
04.79	LS 269, 276, 282, 288, 290, 291, 293, 296 (**T**)
05.79	LS 280 (**MH**)
06.79	LS 215 (**HL**), LS 298, 299, 310, 311 (**MH**), LS 300-307 (**PR**)
07.79	LS 308, 312-315, 317, 319-321, 323, 325, 327 (**HD**)
08.79	LS 316, 318, 322, 326, 329-333, 335-341, 343-345, 347, 349 (**HD**)
09.79	LS 328, 351, 352 (**HD**), LS 381 (**AV**)
	LS 346, 348, 350, 353, 355-359, 361, 363, 365, 366, 368, 370, 378, 379 (**TB**)
10.79	LS 360, 374, 383, 385, 386, 388-391, 393-396, 400, 401, 414 (**TB**)
11.79	LS 324, 364, 375, 377, 384, 402, 404-407 (**D**), LS 334, 354, 376, 380, 399, 403 (**WH**)
	LS 342, 387, 408, 409, 411, 415, 419-421, 427, 431, 433, 435 (**HT**), LS 373, 410 (**NB**)
12.79	LS 382 (**HD**), LS 398, 424 (**HT**), LS 422, 437 (**PR**), LS 423 (**T**),
	LS 425, 432 (**AV**), LS 428, 430 (**RD**)
01.80	LS 362, 367, 372, 392, 416, 417, 434, 436 (**NS**)
02.80	LS 397, 412, 413 (**NS**)
03.80	LS 418 (**AV**), LS 426 (**PR**)
04.81	LS 439-441, 445-455, 457-460, 462-467, 470 (**AG**), LS 443 (**GM**)
05.81	LS 444, 468, 469, 471-476, 478-486, 488-493 (**GM**)
	LS 495-501, 503-506 (**WL**)
06.81	LS 442, 456, 461, 494, 502 (**WL**)
07.81	LS 471 (**AG**), LS 477 (**WL**)
08.81	LS 438 (**WL**)

Overhauls at Aldenham

05.79	**In:**	LS 1
06.80	**In:**	LS 2
08.80	**In:**	LS 3, 4
	Out:	LS 1
09.80	**In:**	LS 6
10.80	**In:**	LS 5
	Out:	LS 2, 3
11.80	**Out:**	LS 4, 6
01.81	**Out:**	LS 5
04.81	**In:**	LS 8
07.81	**In:**	LS 9, 11, 12, 14
08.81	**In:**	LS 13
10.81	**In:**	LS 15, 19, 62, 64, 97
	Out:	LS 2, 3
11.81	**In:**	LS 20, 115, 116, 117
12.81	**Out:**	LS 8, 9, 11, 12, 97
01.82	**In:**	LS 10, 16, 56, 58-60, 82, 85, 108, 118, 119
02.82	**In:**	LS 24, 37, 70, 104, 139, 160, 233
03.82	**In:**	LS 49, 94, 107, 114, 138, 169
	Out:	LS 10, 13
04.82	**In:**	LS 30, 48, 80, 91, 99, 103, 105, 110, 125, 131, 208
	Out:	LS 14, 15, 19, 20, 24, 56, 58, 62, 64, 70, 82, 85, 108, 115-118, 233
05.82	**In:**	LS 27, 71, 72, 98, 129, 134, 136
	Out:	LS 16, 59, 138, 160
06.82	**In:**	LS 28, 36, 69, 95, 149, 174, 222, 236, 265
	Out:	LS 37, 49, 60, 114, 119, 139
07.82	**In:**	LS 47, 65, 74, 137, 223, 226, 229, 230
	Out:	LS 30, 99, 103, 104, 107, 125, 131
08.82	**In:**	LS 35, 76, 90, 101, 251
	Out:	LS 48, 72, 80, 91, 94, 110
09.82	**In:**	LS 23, 33, 42, 63, 68, 79, 111, 133, 155, 162, 204, 205, 221, 334, 354, 376
	Out:	LS 27, 71, 98, 105, 129, 134, 136, 137, 149, 169, 208, 236
10.82	**In:**	LS 18, 29, 51, 73, 78, 83, 87, 100, 127, 157, 240, 300, 301
	Out:	LS 36, 47, 69, 74, 101, 174, 223

11.82	In:	LS 43, 44, 46, 92, 96, 106, 109, 132, 143, 209, 232, 254, 272, 375, 380, 384, 399, 402, 403, 405
	Out:	LS 23, 28, 42, 65, 76, 90, 95, 133, 205, 222, 226, 229, 230, 265, 334, 354, 376
12.82	In:	LS 54, 86, 121, 196, 242, 258, 295, 358
	Out:	LS 33, 35, 63, 68, 79, 87, 111, 155, 157, 162, 204, 221, 240, 251, 301
01.83	In:	LS 25, 32, 45, 84, 161, 168, 176, 186, 207, 238, 244, 246, 257, 364, 377, 407
	Out:	LS 18, 46, 51, 73, 78, 83, 100, 106, 109, 127, 132, 309, 300, 380
02.83	In:	LS 22, 52, 89, 148, 179, 194, 252
	Out:	LS 29, 43, 44, 96, 143, 196, 254, 272, 295, 375, 384, 399, 402, 403
03.83	In:	LS 38, 55, 75, 88, 120, 130, 141, 150, 154, 158, 178, 187, 190, 206, 211, 219, 237, 281, 389
	Out:	LS 45, 54, 92, 121, 161, 176, 232, 238, 242, 244, 257, 258, 358, 407
04.83	In:	LS 213
	Out:	LS 25, 32, 52, 84, 86, 88, 207, 246, 364, 377
05.83	In:	LS 41, 142, 156, 164, 172, 184, 200, 203, 214, 227, 247, 256, 296, 298
	Out:	LS 22, 75, 148, 158, 168, 178, 179, 186, 190, 194, 206, 211, 252, 389
06.83	In:	LS 26, 77, 122, 123, 145, 147, 331
	Out:	LS 38, 55, 89, 120, 130, 141, 150, 154, 213, 281
07.83	In:	LS 112, 128, 151, 167, 182, 264, 297
	Out:	LS 142, 156, 164, 184, 187, 219, 237, 247
08.83	In:	LS 153, 180, 197, 243, 260, 270, 290, 303, 326, 339
	Out:	LS 41, 172, 200, 203, 214, 227, 256, 298
09.83	In:	LS 7, 40, 53, 93, 165, 171, 181, 188, 191-193, 267
	Out:	LS 26, 77, 122, 123, 145, 151, 182, 296, 331
10.83	In:	LS 21, 39, 50, 113, 183, 199, 228, 291, 332
	Out:	LS 112, 128, 147, 167 180, 264, 290, 297, 339
11.83	In:	LS 17, 57, 66, 124, 135, 140, 159, 170, 177, 216, 225, 285, 340
	Out:	LS 40, 93, 153, 153, 243, 270, 303, 326
12.83	In:	LS 34, 126, 163, 173, 189, 195, 215, 220, 277, 324
	Out:	LS 7, 53, 165, 171, 181, 188, 191, 193, 197, 260, 267
01.84	In:	LS 241, 250, 279, 289, 322, 328, 366, 387, 393, 437
	Out:	LS 21, 39, 183, 192, 199, 291, 332
02.84	In:	LS 175, 201, 224, 231, 249, 261, 268, 275, 284, 287, 314, 422
	Out:	LS 17, 50, 113, 126, 225, 228
03.84	In:	LS 61, 67, 81, 166, 202, 245, 248, 253, 255, 259, 309, 360
	Out:	LS 57, 124, 135, 140, 159, 170, 173, 189, 215, 216, 220, 250, 288, 289, 322, 366, 393
04.84	In:	LS 146, 152, 218, 234, 266, 276, 294, 320, 321, 378, 401
	Out:	LS 66, 201, 231, 241, 249, 261, 279, 284, 287, 314, 324, 348, 387, 437
05.84	In:	LS 198, 239, 274, 286, 292, 308, 310, 317, 369
	Out:	LS 67, 166, 175, 224, 245, 255, 259, 275, 360, 422
06.84	In:	LS 102, 210, 235, 262, 271, 273, 282, 283, 293, 307, 315, 319
	Out:	LS 146, 202, 253, 276, 294, 309, 401
07.84	In:	LS 144, 263, 278, 280, 304, 316, 325, 338
	Out:	LS 152, 218, 234, 248, 266, 274, 308, 320, 321, 378
08.84	In:	LS 212, 217, 299, 306, 341, 347, 353, 365, 415, 430
	Out:	LS 163, 177, 239, 286, 310, 317, 369
09.84	In:	LS 269, 346, 350-352, 363, 373
	Out:	LS 34, 198, 277, 285, 292
10.84	In:	LS 288, 311, 318, 327, 329, 330, 361, 371, 374, 381, 385, 390, 414, 421, 432
	Out:	LS 102, 144, 195, 210, 235, 262, 263, 271, 278, 280, 282, 283, 293, 307, 315, 316, 319, 325, 340
11.84	In:	LS 302, 305, 313, 323, 356, 386, 388, 392, 396, 397, 400, 406, 408, 409, 424, 425, 429
	Out:	LS 212, 217, 273, 299, 304, 306, 338, 341, 430
12.84	In:	LS 31, 342, 410, 411, 423, 428
	Out:	LS 347, 350-353, 365
01.85	In:	LS 343, 419, 431
	Out:	LS 269, 373, 415
02.85	In:	LS 417, 436
	Out:	LS 346, 363, 374
03.85	In:	LS
	Out:	LS 288, 318, 329, 330, 371, 381, 385, 390, 414, 421
04.85	In:	LS 312, 355, 427, 434, 460
	Out:	LS 302, 311, 327, 361, 388, 425, 432
05.85	In:	LS 333, 335-337, 344, 348, 349, 359, 362, 368, 370, 379, 383, 391, 394, 395, 398, 404, 412, 413, 416, 418, 426, 433
	Out:	LS 305, 323, 356, 397, 400, 424, 429
06.85	In:	LS 345, 357, 367, 465
	Out:	LS 313, 386, 392, 396, 406, 409, 410

07.85	In:	LS 449, 455, 494
	Out:	LS 31, 342, 408, 411, 423, 428, 434
08.85	In:	LS 443, 477
	Out:	LS 312, 333, 379, 417, 419, 431, 455, 460
09.85	In:	LS 444
	Out:	LS 336, 355, 362, 394, 398, 412, 427
10.85	In:	LS 8, 9, 83, 105, 372, 441, 451, 470, 474
	Out:	LS 348, 368, 395, 413, 494
11.85	In:	LS 46, 48, 60, 106, 420, 472, 473
	Out:	LS 8, 335, 337, 349, 359, 370, 383, 391, 404, 449, 477
12.85	Out:	LS 83, 345, 416, 433, 444
01.86	Out:	LS 105, 343, 344, 367, 372, 442, 443
02.86	Out:	LS 9, 48, 106, 357, 418, 426
03.86	Out:	LS 60, 420, 451, 470, 472-474

Contract overhauls

By British Leyland, Nottingham, 02.85-05.86
LSs 11, 12, 27, 36, 42, 47, 56, 63, 65, 71, 72, 76, 79, 87, 91, 94, 97, 98, 100, 101, 108, 160, 382, 435, 440, 447, 453, 459, 463, 464, 483-485, 488, 492, 497
Total: 36

By Eastern Coach Works, Lowestoft, 04.85-06.85
LSs 441, 450, 456
Total: 3

By Midland Red, Carlyle Works, Birmingham, 10.85-01.86
LSs 28, 30, 33, 372
Total: 4

By Kent Engineering Ltd, Canterbury, 11.85-01.86
LS 90
Total: 1

Contract Overhauls By Date

02.85	In:	LS 447, 453, 497 (*British Leyland*)
04.85	In:	LS 441, 450, 456 (*ECW*)
	Out:	LS 447, 453, 497 (*British Leyland*)
05.85	In:	LS 440, 463 (*British Leyland*)
06.85	In:	LS 492 (*British Leyland*)
	Out:	LS 441, 450, 456 (*ECW*)
07.85	Out:	LS 440, 463 (*British Leyland*)
08.85	Out:	LS 492 (*British Leyland*)
10.85	In:	LS 11, 36, 65, 72, 94, 98, 101, 108 (*British Leyland*)
		LS 28, 30, 33, 372 (*Midland Red*)
11.85	In:	LS 12, 91 (*British Leyland*)
		LS 90 (*Kent Engineering*)
12.85	In:	LS 27, 47, 71, 87, 435 (*British Leyland*)
01.86	In:	LS 42, 56, 63, 79, 97, 100, 382 (*British Leyland*)
	Out:	LS 11, 36, 65, 72, 91, 94, 101, 108 (*British Leyland*)
		LS 28, 30, 372 (*Midland Red*)
		LS 90 (*Kent Engineering*)
02.86	In:	LS 76, 160, 459, 483, 484, 485 (*British Leyland*)
	Out:	LS 12, 98 (*British Leyland*)
		LS 33 (*Midland Red*)
03.86	In:	LS 488 (*British Leyland*)
	Out:	LS 42, 47, 87, 100 (*British Leyland*)
04.86	In:	LS 464 (*British Leyland*)
	Out:	LS 27, 63, 71, 76, 97, 382, 435, 459, 483 (*British Leyland*)
05.86	Out:	LS 56, 160, 464, 484, 485, 488 (*British Leyland*)

Sold

05.85	LS 1, 2, 5
06.85	LS 4
08.85	LS 3
04.86	LS 15, 22
05.86	LS 23
10.86	LS 16, 185
02.87	LS 68, 274, 309, 371
04.87	LS 32, 283, 295, 296, 339, 364
12.87	LS 6
05.88	LS 19, 92, 147, 162, 167, 250, 287, 326, 338, 345, 380, 433
07.88	LS 436
12.88	LS 74
01.89	LS 155, 282, 328
02.89	LS 69
03.89	LS 420
05.89	LS 221, 229, 353
06.89	LS 12, 51
07.89	LS 36, 172, 187, 211, 289, 353
08.89	LS 210, 219, 378
09.89	LS 21, 31, 126, 137, 141, 171, 207, 213, 214, 220, 255
10.89	LS 192, 202, 217, 223, 235, 239, 252, 290
11.89	LS 52, 80, 254, 377, 401
12.89	LS 17, 26
01.90	LS 240
02.90	LS 10, 38, 42, 43, 47, 63, 85, 86, 101, 143, 163, 181, 209, 260, 272, 284, 327, 342, 370
03.90	LS 8, 53, 78, 94, 144, 151, 158, 170, 175, 193, 205, 215, 222, 228, 236, 347, 365, 418
04.90	LS 70, 100, 154, 166, 200, 318, 389
05.90	LS 46, 55, 75, 76, 127, 134, 165, 203
06.90	LS 44, 60, 83, 136, 142, 258, 277, 280, 319, 384, 400, 414
07.90	LS 18, 25, 37, 54, 56, 59, 77, 93, 113, 118, 125, 129, 148, 174, 178, 198, 238, 262, 281, 286, 302, 392, 398, 404, 410
08.90	LS 104, 300, 425
09.90	LS 49, 72, 95, 103, 109, 182, 212, 232, 437
10.90	LS 146, 152, 188, 273, 279, 286, 316, 336, 374-376, 430
11.90	LS 45, 124, 132, 164, 168, 194, 224, 269, 310, 333, 361, 362, 390, 416, 423, 427
12.90	LS 64, 107, 114, 133, 169, 183, 199, 208, 265, 271, 303, 307, 340, 351, 368, 388, 399, 417, 421
01.91	LS 82, 120, 130, 186, 231, 233, 267, 285, 315, 372, 386, 426
02.91	LS 50, 87, 135, 184, 196, 237, 294, 409, 428
03.91	LS 28, 33, 34, 39, 73, 89, 110, 111, 140, 197, 225, 234, 241, 246, 248, 249, 253, 278, 299, 301, 311, 321, 325, 331, 332, 344, 346, 354, 359, 394, 402, 415, 432
04.91	LS 81, 102, 106, 190, 230, 292, 305, 306, 312, 350, 355, 360, 387, 391, 424
05.91	LS 11, 115, 131, 138, 242, 276, 313, 323, 341, 357, 369, 393, 419
06.91	LS 180, 298, 322
07.91	LS 159, 244
09.91	LS 119, 343
10.91	LS 358
11.91	LS 48, 62, 226
12.91	LS 128, 263, 266
01.92	LS 41, 145, 149, 264, 275, 317, 330
02.92	LS 67, 157, 161, 206, 329, 379
03.92	LS 40, 90, 349
04.92	LS 204, 216, 270, 348, 366, 367, 382
05.92	LS 291
06.92	LS 57, 91, 189, 324, 406, 407, 412
07.92	LS 314, 352
08.92	LS 58, 65, 117, 160, 173, 192
09.92	LS 20, 108, 191, 218
10.92	LS 247
11.92	LS 261
01.93	LS 179
03.93	LS 66, 334
05.93	LS 176, 288, 383, 413
06.93	LS 9, 122, 201, 243
07.93	LS 27, 71
09.93	LS 177

12.93	LS 435
01.94	LS 79, 156
04.94	LS 61, 397
05.94	LS 320, 396
07.94	LS 454, LSL 1
08.94	LS 462
09.94	LS 441, 494
10.94	LS 256, 456, 457, 475
11.94	LS 105, 293, 447, 461, 465, 475
12.94	LS 139, 334
01.95	(**MTL London Northern**) LS 464, 485, 488, 489
11.95	(**Stagecoach East London**) LS 121, 308, 403
	(**Centrewest**) GLS 2
11.96	(**London General**) LS 445, 453, 482
12.96	(**Centrewest**) LS 451, 458, 495
02.97	(**Centrewest**) LS 484
12.97	(**Westlink**) LS 13, 30, 97, 98, 116, 408, 434
04.98	(**Westlink**) LS 29
05.98	(**Centrewest**) LS 470, 497
	(**Westlink**) LS 251
06.98	(**Westlink**) LS 24
07.98	(**Westlink**) LS 112
08.98	(**Westlink**) LS 35, 422
10.98	(**Westlink**) LS 7, 88, 123, 150, 245, 259
11.98	(**Westlink**) LS 363, 381
04.99	(**Centrewest**) LS 503
05.99	(**Centrewest**) LS 444
08.99	(**Centrewest**) LS 472
10.99	(**London United**) LS 304
12.99	(**London United**) LS 84, 96, 99, 268, 335, 337, 395
01.00	(**London United**) LS 195, 227, 373, 385
05.00	(**Arriva Kent Thameside**) LS 202, 290, LSL 2
	(**London United**) LS 411, 429
07.00	(**First Capital**) LS 454
09.00	(**Centrewest**) LS 504
07.01	(**London General**) GLS 463, 466, 486
03.02	(**London General**) GLS 501
05.02	(**London General**) GLS 439, 442, 449, 450, 452, 459, 468, 469, 471, 474, 476, 478, 481, 483, 490, 491, 493, 499, 502, 505
08.02	(**London General**) GLS 448, 500
09.02	(**London General**) GLS 438, 443, 477, 487, 496
12.02	(**London General**) GLS 440, 446, 455, 460, 467, 473, 479, 480, 492, 498, 506
05.03	(**London United**) LS 405
06.03	(**London Sovereign**) LS 153
12.04	(**London United**) LS 297, 431

Dispersal upon privatisation of LBL, 1994:

To Westlink, 20.01.94
LS 7, 13, 24, 29, 30, 35, 84, 88, 96-99, 112, 116, 123, 150, 153, 195, 227, 245, 251, 259, 268, 297, 304, 335, 337, 363, 373, 381, 385, 395, 405, 408, 411, 422, 429, 431, 434
LSs 84, 153, 268, 373, 405 and 429 used by West Midlands Travel from 09.94 but re-acquired 09.95
Fleet subsequently acquired by West Midlands Travel on 11.04.94 and then by London United 15.09.95

To Centrewest, 02.09.94
LS 444, 451, 458, 470, 472, 484, 495, 497, 503, 504
GLS 2

To Stagecoach East London, 06.09.94
LS 121, 308, 403

To London General, 02.11.94
LS 445, 453, 482
GLS 1, 438-440, 442, 443, 446, 448-450, 455, 459, 460, 463, 467-469, 471, 473, 474, 476-481, 483, 486, 487, 490-493, 496, 498, 499-502, 505, 506

To MTL London Northern, 26.10.94
LS 464, 485, 488, 489

Former LSs reappearing on tendered routes with new operators:

Boro'Line Maidstone:	LS 162, 345, 380, 436 (as 901-904);
	Loaned from Eastbourne, 1989; LS 68, 274, 309, 339, 371 (as 17, 18, 20-22)
London & Country:	LS 425 (as National Greenway 342 (SIB 6712))
Ensignbus:	LS 1 (as 502)
Capital Citybus:	LS 176 (as 736), 256 (as 798), 288 (as 737), 396 (as 756), 454 (as 794, subsequently 744), LSL 1 (as 797)
	Loaned from Volvo, 1993: LS 190
Kentish Bus:	LS 192, 202 (subsequently 202, 493, 3493), 290 (subsequently 290, 494, 3494), LSL 2 (subsequently 42, 492, 3492)
	Also loaned; LS 105, 320

Garages and routes operated by London Transport and successors

Garage (code)	Start date	Finish date	Routes operated (unscheduled in italics)
Ash Grove (**AG**)	25.04.81	23.11.91	*106,* 236, 501, 502, 513, '555', '556', D6, S3
Streatham (**AK**)	11.90	11.90	*115*
Merton (**AL**)	04.09.82	26.01.89	57, 115, 127, 152, *156,* 163, 189
	06.89	06.89	*57*
Hounslow (**AV**)	15.08.76	03.92	27, 82, *91,* 98, 110, 111, 116, 117, *120, 140,* 202, 203, 203A, *232, 237,* 257(i), A1(i), *E4, H21, H22, H23, H24,* H37, *H98, N11*
	04.04.96	07.99	*81,* 110, 111, 116, *120,* 92235(ii), *H22, H32,* H37, *H91, H98*
Bow (**BW**)	02.11.85	16.01.88	8, 108, D1
Bexleyheath (**BX**)	16.01.88	03.91	*96, 99, 178, 229,* 244(ii), *269, 272, 291, 401,* 422, *469,* 492
Chalk Farm (**CF**)	22.03.89	09.11.91	*46,* 168, 214, Z1
Dalston (**D**)	19.11.73	13.06.76	S2
	21.05.78	25.04.81	236, S2
Enfield (**E**)	03.90	01.92	*121, 144A, 191*
Elmers End (**ED**)	19.06.77	25.10.86	12A, 12B, *54, 75,* 194, 194A, 289
Fulwell (**FW**)	09.04.78	27.09.80	90, 110
Victoria (**GM**)	09.05.81	15.08.87	500, 507, 639
Harrow Weald (**HD**)	22.10.78	19.01.91	114, 136, *140, 183,* 201(ii), 209, 211(ii), 258, 340, H1
Hanwell (**HL**)	17.09.78	06.81	*E1, E2,* E3
Holloway (**HT**)	18.06.78	01.91	*17,* 210, 239, *271, C11*
Kingston (**K**)	27.06.87	11.98	*131,* 213S, 216, 371, *371S,* 411, 468, K2, K3
Loughton (**L**)	22.07.78	24.05.86	20, 20A, 167, 179, 201(i), 206, 250, 250A, 254(i), 254(ii), 255(i)
Muswell Hill (**MH**)	18.06.78	21.06.86	210, 244(i)
Norbiton (**NB**)	31.03.79	30.11.87	*65, 71, 72, 85,* 131, *211*(i), *213,* 215, 216, 218, 219, 306
	02.88	18.09.90	*85,* 200, *213,* K10, *X71*
North Street (**NS**)	05.01.80	27.07.81	*103,* 247, *247B, 294*
Potters Bar (**PB**)	27.10.86	07.89	*84, 107,* 242, *263,* 310A, *W8*
	21.07.90	22.09.90	*W8*
Peckham (**PM**)	04.11.78	06.90	*63,* 70, 70A, 78, P2, P3, P5, N85, N86
Poplar (**PR**)	22.04.78	02.11.85	108, 173, 276, D1, S2
Walworth (**RA**)	15.08.87	28.10.90	500, 501, 502, 503, 505, 506, 507, 509, 510, 513
Waterloo (**RA**)	28.10.90	01.06.02	*11, 211,* 501, 502, 503, 505, 507, 510, 511, 513, 521
Hornchurch (**RD**)	26.02.78	24.09.88	*193,* 244(ii), 246, 246A, 248, 248A, 252, 256, X99
Shepherd's Bush (**S**)	01.07.89	06.01.90	283
Stockwell (**SW**)	29.01.83	02.11.85	115, *170,* P4
Leyton (**T**)	18.05.78	09.90	*38, 48,* 55, 97, 97A, 179, 179A, 206, 230, 235(i), 236, *257*(ii), 275, N96
Bromley (**TB**)	21.08.77	29.02.92	1, 61, *119,* 126, 138, 146, *208,* 227, 261, 284, 338, 471, B1, R5
Croydon (**TC**)	17.04.82	16.02.84	*166A,* 234, 234A
	25.11.86	06.91	12A, 12B, *50, 68,* 115, *130,* 166, *166A, 190*(i), 194, 194A, 254(iii), 255(ii), 289, *366, 403*
Thornton Heath (**TH**)	09.90	05.91	*412*
Catford (**TL**)	27.10.84	29.07.89	108B, 124, 160, 181, L1, L2
Uxbridge (**UX**)	07.09.80	12.10.96	98, 128, 128A, 204, *207,* 222, 223, 224, 607, U1, *U4*
Turnham Green (**V**)	17.09.78	10.05.80	E3
Stamford Brook (**V**)	10.05.80	21.05.81	E3
	07.90	08.93	*27, 190*(ii), *237,* 283, *391,* A1(ii), A2
Cricklewood (**W**)	05.02.78	31.05.86	268
	14.02.87	17.11.90	32, 112, *205,* 245
West Ham (**WH**)	24.11.79	06.92	8, 8A, 10, 56, 108, 173, 241, *262, 262A,* 276, 278, 299, D1, D3, D4, D5, D6, D7, *S1,* S2, S3
Hounslow Heath (**WK**)*	09.08.86	03.08.99	*81,* 110, 116, 117, 203, 216, *H22, H23, H91*
Wood Green (**WN**)	01.89	03.90	*41, 141, 144A,* 221, *W2*
Walworth (**WL**)**	08.06.81	02.11.85	501

* HH from 1998
** see also RA

Garages and routes operated by tendered contractors

Ensignbus

Dagenham (**DM**)	24.09.88	02.89	*165, 246, 446*

Capital Citybus (First Capital from 03.07.98)

Dagenham (**DM**)	05.93	06.00	*1, 123, 165, 215, 246, 248, 252, 257, 296, 345, 365, 396, 446, 511, 645, 652, D6*
Northumberland Park (**NP**)*	05.94	05.96	*212, 257, 298*

* Loans from Dagenham

Boro'Line Maidstone

Crayford	11.88	03.91	*132, 228, 328, 422, 492*

London & Country (Londonlinks from 01.01.95)

Walworth (**WL**)	02.01.93	11.96	*78, 85*, P3

Mobility Buses

London Buses Ltd

Ash Grove (**AG**)	28.10.85	28.03.88	921, 922, 923, 924, 925(i), 926, 927, 928, 947, 948, 966, 973
Clapton (**CT**)	23.11.91	20.06.92	921, 922, 923, 924, 925(ii), 927, 929
Harrow Weald (**HD**)	19.01.91	30.11.92	981, 982, 983, 984, 985, 986, 987, 988, 989
North Street (**NS**)*	27.10.90	28.10.95	900, 901, 906, 907, 908, 909, 910, 920, 947, 948, 951, 952, 953, 954, 955, 956, 957, 958, 959, 960, 961, 966, 973
Leyton (**T**)	27.11.84	23.11.91	900, 901, 902, 903(i), 904, 905, 906, 907, 908, 909, 910, 921, 922, 923, 924, 925(i), 925(ii), 926(i), 927, 928, 929, 947, 948, 966, 973
Peckham (**PM**)**	27.06.87	26.02.94	931, 932, 933, 936, 937, 970, 971, 972
Cricklewood (**W**)	01.08.88	19.01.91	981, 982, 983, 984, 985, 986, 987, 988, 989

* Occasional forays to routes 247, 345 and 499; Stagecoach East London from 06.10.94; network operated from Barking April-June 1995
** Relocated premises from 29.01.94

Kentish Bus

Northfleet (**NF**)	26.03.90	31.03.00	911, 912, 913, 914, 915, 916, 917, 918, 919, 926(ii), 928, 930, 934

Capital Citybus

Northumberland Park (**NP**)*	20.06.92	18.06.94	900, 901, 903 (ii), 906, 907, 908, 909, 910, 920, 921, 922, 923, 924, 925(ii), 927, 929, 947, 948, 951, 952, 953, 954, 955, 956, 957, 958, 959, 960, 961, 966, 973

* Also visited routes 153, 215 and loaned to Dagenham to visit routes 246, 365

Out-county, council contract and commercial services operated

Surrey:	216, 218, 416, 417, 436, 468, 501, 536, 566, 567, 568, 569, 572, 578, 582, 833 (**Westlink**)
	109/405 (**Panther Travel**)
	555, 556 (**London United**)
Essex:	265 (**Blue Triangle**)
	500 (**LBL**)
	323, 324, 348 (**Capital Citybus / First Capital**)
Hertfordshire:	U1 (**LBL / Centrewest**)
	310A, 318 (**LBL**)
Middlesex:	398 (**Scorpio Coaches**)

BIBLIOGRAPHY

Books

The London Bus Review of … (REV) (1973-1992), LOTS 1974-1994
Reshaping London's Buses, Barry Arnold & Mike Harris, Capital Transport 1982
London Transport Buses, Capital Transport 1977-1984
London Bus Handbook, Capital Transport 1985-2002
London Bus Handbook, part 2: Independents, Capital Transport 1987-1990
London Transport Scrapbook for … (1976-1980), Capital Transport 1977-1981
The London Bus Diary 1991/92, R. J. Waterhouse, TPC 1992.
Bus Monographs 2: Leyland National, Stephen Morris, Ian Allan 1984
London Transport in the 1980s, Michael H. C. Baker, Ian Allan 2008
Privatising London's Buses, Roger Torode, Capital Transport 2015

Magazines, Supplements, Articles and Periodicals

The London Bus (TLB), LOTS, monthly
The London Bus Extra (TEX), LOTS, yearly editions from 1973-1984
London Bus Magazine (LBM), LOTS, quarterly, particularly
    'Twenty Years of the Leyland National' by Chris Atkins in LBM81 (Summer 1992)
BUSES magazine, Ian Allan, monthly
SUP-44A London Bus Disposals – Where are they Now? March 2008, LOTS 2008.
Fleet History LT9; The Vehicles of London Transport and its Predecessors; Modern Classes (RM Class to date),
    PSV Circle 1981.

Websites and Groups

Bus Lists on the Web (www.buslistsontheweb.co.uk)
Ian's Bus Stop – LS (http://www.countrybus.org/National/LS.htm)
London Bus Routes by Ian Armstrong (www.londonbuses.co.uk)